How to Pass

English for Business

Third Level

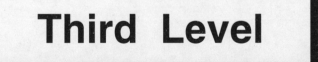

How to Pass English for Business Third Level

Published in 1994

1. Auflage 1994

© **Copyright Logophon Lehrmittel Verlag GmbH**

ISBN 3-922514-32-4

Published by:	Logophon Lehrmittel Verlag
Verlag:	Bonifaziusplatz 4a, 55118 Mainz, Germany
Layout:	Lynne M Evans

Printed and bound in Slovakia.

Other books in this series:

How to Pass English for Business First Level
ISBN 3-922514-30-8

How to Pass English for Business Second Level
ISBN 3-922514-31-6

ACKNOWLEDGEMENTS

The authors would like to thank all those who have helped in writing this book.

Special thanks to Bernard Bater and Sally Wade at the LCCIEB, to Jean-Pierre Jouteux, Pierre Semidei and Gabi Schaub at Logophon.

Many thanks also to John and Lucy Davison, Astrid Feistel, Anna Silanova and Lynne Evans.

Last but not least, thanks to the Euro-Schule Gera and all the students who are now proud owners of an LCCIEB "English for Business" Third Level Certificate.

FOREWORD

Peter Godwin CBE

I am delighted to commend this book to assist students in attaining success in English for Business.

With English recognised as the world's transactional language, an ability to use it fluently represents a considerable advantage and the London Chamber of Commerce and Industry certificate has become recognised as an international passport to employment.

The LCCI Examinations Board was set up over a hundred years ago to provide qualifications created **by** the business community **for** the business community. It is now at the forefront of vocational education and dovolopmont, oporating in moro than 00 countrieo throughout the world.

English for Business focuses heavily on practical and realistic communicative tasks in a work environment. Support materials will prove vital to both teachers and candidates worldwide in achieving good results. I believe that this new series of textbooks on "How to Pass English for Business" will provide excellent, clear, systematic guidelines to help candidates achieve their aims and, in this increasingly qualification-led world, an LCCIEB certificate in English for Business can give an undoubted edge to those wishing to operate in international business circles.

Peter Godwin CBE
Managing Director, West Merchant Bank Limited
Chairman, Asia Pacific Advisory Group

FOREWORD

Both teachers and students will welcome the publication of this volume of assignments designed to provide practice material for those who are preparing for the LCCIEB's Third Level English for Business examination. Since the assignments deal with realistic business situations, this material is equally suitable for those who are studying the use of English in business, but who are not being prepared for LCCIEB examinations.

The authors have used texts of past LCCIEB examinations as their base material. This means that teachers and students will acquire familiarity with the format of examination assignments and the business practices underlying them.

Students should be encouraged to use their knowledge of business practices and the language of business in order to tackle the problems set out in this book. The specimen solutions provided by the authors illustrate these principles admirably.

Ernest V Lee
Director of Examinations
LCCIEB

Contents

This book is for candidates preparing for the Third Level of the London Chamber of Commerce and Industry Examinations Board English for Business Examination.

It can be used either as a class book or for self-study. It contains 5 sections which look at those tasks which are likely to come up in the examination, namely:

* Letters
* Reports
* Short Answers
* Memos
* Miscellaneous

At the back of the book there is an **Answer Key**.

Each section has an Introduction which explains to the student how to approach the question.

The sections on Letters, Reports, Memos and Miscellaneous questions are divided up and take the student through the following 6 stages:

* Identify the Task
* Layout
* Identify Relevant Information
* Group/Order Relevant Information
* Write the Answer
* Check the Answer

Practice 1 provides the student with an example of how to complete the task. In each subsequent practice the student has to complete one more stage. By Practice 7 the student completes all the stages alone.

Three questions are then provided as further practice and suggested answers to all the practice questions can be found at the back of the book.

	STAGES					
	1	2	3	4	5	6
Practice 1	○	○	○	○	○	○
Practice 2	○	○	○	○	○	□
Practice 3	○	○	○	○	□	□
Practice 4	○	○	○	□	□	□
Practice 5	○	○	□	□	□	□
Practice 6	○	□	□	□	□	□
Practice 7	□	□	□	□	□	□
Practice 8	□	□	□	□	□	□
Practice 9	□	□	□	□	□	□
Practice 10	□	□	□	□	□	□

○ Stages already completed.   Student completes stage. □

The section on Short Answers is divided up and takes the student through the following 4 stages:

* Identify the Task
* What to do Before you Start
* Write the Answer
* Check the Answer

INTRODUCTION

Practice 1 provides the student with an example of how to complete the task. In each subsequent practice the student has to complete one more stage. By Practice 5 the student completes all the stages alone.

Five questions are then provided as further practice and suggested answers to all the practice questions can be found at the back of the book.

	STAGES			
	1	**2**	**3**	**4**
Practice 1	○	○	○	○
Practice 2	○	○	○	□
Practice 3	○	○	□	□
Practice 4	○	□	□	□
Practice 5	□	□	□	□
Practice 6	□	□	□	□
Practice 7	□	□	□	□
Practice 8	□	□	□	□
Practice 9	□	□	□	□
Practice 10	□	□	□	□

○ Stages already completed.   Student completes stage. □

The Exam

The exam consists of 4 questions, all of which are to be answered. These questions are described by the LCCIEB as:

a   "The composition of a letter, the stimulus for which will be an incoming letter, or the employer's instructions, or both. The rubric will include data on which a reply might be based and an indication of the tone required. The candidate's letter must be "mailable" and hence must be correctly laid out, linguistically accurate and appropriate in tone and content.

(25 marks)

b   The drafting of an internal report based on raw data given in the form of graphs, notes, press cuttings, charts, tables, etc. Candidates will have to understand, select, collate and, if necessary, supplement this data in order to write the report in the light of the instructions given. The report must be clear, well organised and logically paragraphed and - where appropriate - numbered. The language must be correct and stylistically appropriate, so that the report will be fit for internal distribution. The rubric will give guidance on the form and content required

(25 marks)

c   A comprehension task in which candidates will be asked to show understanding of a passage for a defined purpose. This might be a press article, an extract from a business journal, company report, circular letter, tender, or some other form of business reading matter, with which candidates should be familiar at this stage. Questions will be asked to probe their understanding, not only of factual content but of argument, bias, persuasive devices and internal organisation. Their comprehension should be signalled by the most economic means available, eg incomplete sentences, figures, single words, diagrams, organisation trees, etc

(25 marks)

d   A conversion task involving the reformulation of a message for some defined purpose. Thus candidates may be required to produce a memo from a telex, cable, letter or computer printout; or an abstract from an article; or a summary of a phone call for discussion; or a telex/telegram/cable from a company notice, employer's instructions, etc.

The essential is that a message received in one form is transmitted in another form. This will involve reducing lengthy messages, expanding fragmentary messages, completing inadequate messages, or selecting from redundant messages. In transferring the data from one form to the other the candidate must adopt the appropriate format and tone."

(25 marks)

Oral Test

"Candidates whose mother tongue is not English will be required to pass an Oral Test before they can be awarded a certificate. The Oral Test will consist of a conversation (8-10 minutes) with the examiner." The topics discussed include current affairs, economic issues, etc and the candidate is expected to have a good grasp of commercial or technical terminology relating to his/her occupation.

Certificates will be awarded only to those who pass both the Written and Oral Tests.

Candidates may chose to take the third level (Intermediate), of the LCCIEB's Spoken English for Industry and Commerce Examinations, in place of the Oral Test.

For further information regarding the organisation and administration of English for Business Examinations, contact:

London Chamber of Commerce and Industry Examinations Board
Marlowe House
Station Road
Sidcup
KENT   DA15 7BJ

Tel: 081 302 0261
Fax: 081 309 5169

LONDON *of* CHAMBER
COMMERCE AND INDUSTRY
EXAMINATIONS BOARD

Certificate

This is to certify that

A N OTHER

has been examined by the Examinations Board of the London Chamber of Commerce and Industry and has been found qualified to receive this Certificate for proficiency as shown below.

Third Level Single Subjects

English for Business   Pass****
****

Examinations Series   FOUR 1993   Centre   YTEST /0001

James Duncan

Sir James Duncan
Chairman, Commercial Education Trust

Simon Sperryn

W. J. Swords   Simon Sperryn
Chief Executive of the Examinations Board   Chief Executive of the Chamber

SECTION 1: Letters

Introduction

The letter always occurs in Question 1. The question often provides a letter and some information which are the basis for reply.

Stage 1: Identify the Task

Read the question and work out exactly what you are required to do. The instructions at the bottom of the question normally read "Draft the appropriate letter." or" "Write the correct reply."

Stage 2: Layout

Normal layout.

your company address	- top right hand corner
date	- top right hand corner below sender's address
name and address of recipient	- beneath date on left hand side
correct salutation	- "Dear (name)" - if you know the person's name
	"Dear Sir/Madam" - if you don't know the person's name
	"Dear Sirs" - if you are writing to a company or organisation
subject line	- below the salutation and underlined

complimentary close	- "Yours sincerely" - after "Dear (Name)"
	"Yours faithfully" - after "Dear Sir/Madam" and "Dear Sirs"

Use the letters "pp" or "for" before your signature if you are asked to "write a letter under my name" or "sign it on my behalf". Leave a space if you are asked to "draft a letter ready for my signature".

name	- printed name of sender
position	- beneath printed name and underlined
enclosures	- use "Enc" if necessary

Example of Layout

24 High Street
Newcastle
NE46 4AB

29 March 1993

Mr J Smith
28 Broom Street
Hexham
NE71 2SV

Dear Mr Smith

Proposed Meeting

....
....

Yours sincerely

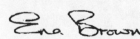

Ena Brown
Sales Manager

Stage 3: Identify Relevant Information

The letter is usually a reply to an incoming letter and/or employer's instructions. Decide exactly what the recipient wants to know and identify the relevant information.

Stage 4: Group/Order Relevant Information

Group the information according to theme and present it in a logical order (from general to specific).

Stage 5: Write the Letter

Language in letters must be business-like and polite. The use of separate paragraphs for different points is recommended.

Stage 6: Check Your Work

1   Have you completed the task?
2   Is your layout correct?
3   Do you have all the correct information?
4   Is it ordered in the best way?
5   Is the language appropriate for a letter?
6   Have you checked spelling, grammar and punctuation?

Practice 1

Andrew Morgan is a Supermarket Manager at the Grantborough Superstore, Ludsby Road, Grantborough, North Lincolnshire, LN3 4BJ. He learns from one of his assistants that they have just received a consignment of food stuffs from regular suppliers in Kent. The assistant is concerned because some of the goods received are in poor condition. He complains...

"Much of the vegetables and fruit is decidedly 'off' See, these bananas; there should be the equivalent of 200lbs - well I wouldn't be surprised if half of them are rotten; and these lettuces, look at them, they're wilting. Anything coming straight from the cold store should be in tip-top condition. It's the same with most of the other goods. Have you ever seen soft raw carrots? The grapefruit, the oranges, and pretty well all the fruit and vegetables are very bad.

Shouldn't be surprised if the vehicle had been loaded for a couple of days and its cooling system - if it had one - had broken down. You cannot tell about the state of fruit until you open the boxes."

The Supermarket Manager tries to get the supplier on the phone but the number has the engaged signal. Andrew writes a sharp letter to the supplier 'to put his comments on record'. His letter refers to the state of the consignment and makes the following points:

You must have known about the state of goods before despatch.

Lets the trade down.

Please replace goods quickly.

Cannot expect payment.

Customers disappointed at having to wait for goods.

Expect future discounts.

Will have to review future trading situation.

Expect a full explanation.

Very disappointed - and if problems, why no phone call?

Write the letter from Andrew Morgan to the suppliers:

J McShane & Co
Harbour Road
Folkestone
CT20 7AK

(Series 1, 1993, Q1)

Stage 1:   Identify the Task

Write the letter.

Stage 2:   Layout

• your address - The Grantborough Superstore, Ludsby Road, Grantborough, North Lincolnshire, LN3 4BJ
• addressee - J McShane and Co, Harbour Road, Folkestone, CT20 7AK
• date - 9 March
• salutation - Dear Sirs
• subject line - Consignment of fruit and vegetables
• close - Yours faithfully
• signature   - signature
  name   - Andrew Morgan
  position   - Supermarket Manager

Stage 3:   Identify Relevant Information

- consignment of foods arrived
- goods in poor condition
- vegetables and fruit 'off', rotten or wilting
- looks like cooling system broke down for 2 days
- despatchers must have known about state of goods
- lets the trade down
- want replacement quickly
- they can't expect payment
- disappointed because have to wait
- expect future discounts
- review situation
- want full explanation
- if there was a problem why didn't they phone?

Stage 4:   Group/Order Relevant Information

1   Consignment of food just arrived.
2   Goods in poor condition.
3   Vegetables and fruit 'off', rotten, wilting or bad.
4   Looks like cooling system broke down.
5   McShane must have known state of goods when despatched.
6   Disappointed because now have to wait.
7   Want replacement quickly.
8   Can't expect payment for this.
9   If there was a problem why didn't they phone?
10 Want a full explanation.
11 Expect future discounts.
12 Lets the trade down.

Stage 5:   Write the Letter

> The Grantborough Superstore
> Ludsby Road
> Grantborough
> North Lincolnshire   LN3 4BJ
>
>
> 9 March 1993
>
>
> J McShane & Co
> Harbour Road
> Folkestone   CT20 7AK
>
>
> Dear Sirs
>
> <u>Consignment of Fruit and Vegetables</u>
>
> I have just received a consignment from you and regret that I must inform you of the poor condition of these goods. Most of the vegetables and fruit are off, rotten, wilting or simply bad. In fact, the whole consignment looks as if it was loaded and then left for two days with no cooling system. Whatever the reason, the state of the goods must have been known to you on despatch.
>
> I am now left in a position where I have no goods to sell. This, as I'm sure you understand is not only disappointing to me, but it could mean that **my** customers may go elsewhere. I need a replacement for this consignment immediately and I do not expect an invoice for the goods. If there was a problem you should have phoned - we are after all, only human.
>
> The situation has arisen, however, and I expect a full explanation of this unpleasant problem. I also expect future discounts if we are to continue working together. Events like this do not just let **our** customers down, they are also bad for the trade.
>
> I am sorry to have to write you in such a tone. Such a situation cannot be allowed to happen again. I look forward to hearing from you in the next few days.
>
> Yours faithfully
>
> *Andrew Morgan*
>
> Andrew Morgan
> <u>Supermarket Manager</u>

Stage 6:   Check your Work

Checklist: Letter

1	Have you completed the task?	☑
2	Is your layout correct?	☑
3	Do you have all the correct information?	☑
4	Is it ordered in the best way?	☑
5	Is the language appropriate for a letter?	☑
6	Have you checked spelling, grammar and punctuation?	☑

Practice 2

Andrew Johnson of McFarlane Engineering, West Kilbride, GL3 7AG, is furious. He says to you, his personal assistant, "Just look at what they've sent us! We had to wait three weeks more than they had promised, now we'll have to wait again - that'll put our production back. Here, look at my order.

McFarlane Engineering
West Kilbride
GL3 7AG

To Engineering Supplies   **Order No** 5731/31
East Humberside
HU3 3AJ

Quantity	Description	Part No	
500	Machine Parts	3704A	They have sent 3074A - ½" smaller!
500	Machine Parts	2763A	This, strangely, is all right.
770	Steel Pipes	P438	Completely wrong, they are too short and too small.
400	Casings	CJ43	No casings sent.
30	Large M/C Bodies	C463	They have sent 40 - more than we have room for.

Signed: *Andrew Johnson*   **Date:**   12 October 1992

The other major part of the order, C76J's, which they promised faithfully for today, won't be available for another two months. What's gone wrong? They've never been like this with previous orders. With our loss of production this is going to cost money - but not **ours**! Check any penalty clauses in the contract for late delivery..."

Write the letter of complaint from Andrew Johnson to: Engineering Supplies
East Humberside
HU3 3AJ

(Series 4, 1992, Q1)

SECTION 1

Stage 1: Identify the Task

Write the letter of complaint.

Stage 2: Layout

- your address - McFarlane Engineering, West Kilbride, GL3 7AG
- addressee - Engineering Supplies, East Humberside, HU3 3AJ
- date - (today's date)
- salutation - Dear Sirs
- subject line - Order No 5731/31
- close - Yours faithfully
- signature - signature
  name   - Andrew Morgan
  position   - Manager

Stage 3: Identify Relevant Information

- received goods
- 3 weeks late already
- don't agree with order
- put our production back
- 500 x 3704A ordered
- received 500 x 3074A
- ½" smaller
- 500 x 2763A arrived okay
- 770 x P438 received are too short and too small
- 400 x CJ43 ordered were not sent at all
- 30 x C463 ordered - 40 sent - we have no room for these
- C76J's promised for today, will not be available for 2 months
- loss of production will cost money
- solicitors looking at penalty clauses in contract
- order no/ref

Stage 4: Group/Order Relevant Information

1   Order number.
2   Received goods.
3   Do not agree with the order.
4   500 machine part 3704A ordered - received 500 x 3074A which is ½" smaller.
5   770 steel pipes P438 ordered and received but they are too short and too small.
6   400 casing CJ43 were ordered - not sent.
7   C76J's not delivered at all, available in two months.
8   What has gone wrong?
9   Loss of production will cost us dearly.
10 Solicitors looking at penalty clauses in contract.
11 Expect immediate reply.
12 What steps you are taking to complete order.
13 Otherwise you will hear from our solicitors.

Stage 5: Write the Letter

McFarlane Engineering
West Kilbride   GL3 7AG

(today's date)

Engineering Supplies
East Humberside   HU3 3AJ

Dear Sirs

Order No 5731/31

We refer to our order number 5731/31. The goods delivered today were already three weeks overdue and now when they finally do arrive they do not agree with our order.

We ordered   500   3704A   you sent 3074A which are ½" smaller.
We ordered   500   2763A   this you got right!
We ordered   770   P438   what you sent are completely different; they are too short and too small.
We ordered   400   CJ43   none of these were received.
We ordered   30   C463   you sent 40 and we have no room to store so many.
We ordered   C76J's   not delivered at all - won't be available for another two months.

What has gone wrong? You have never been this bad with previous orders. The loss of production we are going to experience as a result of this will cost us dearly.

We have instructed our solicitors to look at the penalty clauses in the contract regarding late delivery and will, if necessary, instigate the appropriate steps.

I expect an immediate reply from you to hear what steps you have taken to complete this order, otherwise you will be hearing from our solicitors.

Yours faithfully

Andrew Johnson

Andrew Johnson
Manager

Now complete the following stage.

Stage 6: Check your Work

Checklist: Letter

1   Have you completed the task?   ☐
2   Is your layout correct?   ☐
3   Do you have all the correct information?   ☐
4   Is it ordered in the best way?   ☐
5   Is the language appropriate for a letter?   ☐
6   Have you checked spelling, grammar and punctuation?   ☐

Practice 3

Mr Alec Paxton is munching his way through a meat pie when his teeth come into contact with something hard in the pie. Mr Paxton carefully takes the bits of pie from his mouth to see what has caused the problem. Unfortunately, as he takes the pie from his mouth he realises his is also taking out parts of two teeth that were recently capped by his dentist at a fee approaching £200. He finds that the 'ingredient' in the meat pie was a half inch piece of nail.

Mr Paxton is furious. He decides to write to the manufacturer of the pie - Swaythings Ltd of Tadcaster, Yorks, TA1 3AJ - threatening them with legal action and prosecuting under a variety of Health and Safety Acts, Consumer Protection Acts and a number of other Acts of Parliament. Above all, he wants an apology and immediate compensation for his broken teeth.

Write the letter to the pie manufacturer from the agitated Mr Paxton who lives at:

13 Doncaster Road, Sheffield, South Yorks, S1 4AH

(Series 2, 1992, Q1)

Stage 1: Identify the Task

Write a letter.

Stage 2: Layout

- your address - 13 Doncaster Road, Sheffield, South Yorks, S1 4AH
- addressee - Swaythings Ltd, Tadcaster, Yorks, TA1 3AJ
- date - (today's date)
- salutation - Dear Sirs

- subject line - Meat pie bought in Easterly Supermarket
- close - Yours faithfully
- signature - signature
  name - Alec Paxton
  position - (no position)

Stage 3: Identify Relevant Information

- eating pie
- teeth came into contact with something hard
- loud crack
- carefully takes bits out of mouth to see what it was
- also part of his teeth at same time
- teeth recently capped by dentist
- fee £200
- half inch piece of nail in pie
- furious
- threaten company with legal action and prosecution
- variety of Health and Safety Acts
- Consumer Protection Acts
- number of other Acts of Parliament
- wants apology
- immediate compensation for broken teeth
- take matter further with solicitor
- pie bought last week from Easterly Supermarket in Sheffield
- enclose wrapper and piece of metal
- eating pie for lunch
- what may have happened if swallowed
- your view on matter

Stage 4: Group/Order Relevant Information

1. Last week bough meat pie from Easterly's Supermarket, Sheffield.
2. When eating pie for lunch, bit into something hard.
3. Heard a loud crack.
4. Carefully removed bits of pie plus two teeth I have recently had capped.
5. Week before, paid £200 dentist's bill.
6. Furious.
7. Especially when realised what might have happened if I had swallowed it.
8. Enclose wrapper and piece of metal.
9. Intend to take matter further with solicitor.
10. Health and Safety Acts/Consumer Protection Act and number of Acts of Parliament.
11. Apology.
12. Immediate compensation.
13. Your views on the matter.

Now complete the following stages.

Stage 5:   Write the Letter

Stage 6:   Check your Work ☑

Checklist: Letter

1	Have you completed the task?	☐
2	Is your layout correct?	☐
3	Do you have all the correct information?	☐
4	Is it ordered in the best way?	☐
5	Is the language appropriate for a letter?	☐
6	Have you checked spelling, grammar and punctuation?	☐

SECTION 1

Practice 4

John Farmer, his wife and three children, have rented a boat, a cabin cruiser, for a fortnight to tour the Norfolk Broads. They have responded to an advertisement in the 'Norwich Newsman'. When they go to collect their cruiser at Oulton Broad, they become terribly upset.

"The boat's half in the water", says John.

"It's only half the size they promised", says Mrs Edith Farmer.

"There are only two bunks", chorused the youngsters, beginning to cry.

"There aren't any provisions as promised and nothing to cook anything or heat anything up with - and as for the bathroom and toilet, they're a joke", moaned Edith.

"Make a list of what's wrong", says John Farmer. "I'm going to write the firm a very strong letter indicating that I want our money back - plus compensation - or else I'll broadcast this situation on the BBC and ITV travel programmes. I'll make sure they hear about our problems, especially after our travelling all day by train to get here!"

Write the letter John Farmer sends to: Cruising for Pleasure, Oulton Broad, Norfolk, LO3 4NJ

Mr Farmer's home address is 3 Workington Way, Barrow, Lancs, BA4 4NK.

(Series 3, 1992, Q1)

Stage 1: Identify the Task

Write the letter of complaint.

Stage 2: Layout

- your address - 3 Workington Way, Barrow, Lancs, BA4 4NK
- addressee - Cruising for Pleasure, Oulton Broad, Norfolk, LO3 4NJ
- date - (today's date)
- salutation - Dear Sirs
- subject line - Cabin Cruiser rented at Oulton Broad
- close - Yours faithfully
- signature - signature
  name   - John Farmer
  position   - (no position)

Stage 3: Identify Relevant Information

- booking number
- rented cabin cruiser for 2 week tour of Norfolk Broads
- reply to advertisement in the "Norwich Newsman"
- collect boat at Oulton Broad
- boat half in the water
- only half the size promised
- only two bunks/nothing for the children
- no provisions as promised
- nothing to cook or heat anything up with
- bathroom and toilet a joke
- strong letter of complaint
- want money back plus compensation
- or else broadcast situation BBC and ITV travel programmes
- travelled all day by train to get to Oulton Broad
- representative Mr S Williams unhelpful, said "It is your problem"
- family/children had been looking forward to holiday
- ruined by broken promises
- prompt reply and settlement
- if not you will hear from my solicitor

Now complete the following stages.

Stage 4: Group/Order Relevant Information

....
....
....
....
....
....
....
....
....
....
....
....
....
....
....
....
....
....

Stage 5: Write the Letter

Stage 6: Check your Work ☑

Checklist: Letter

1	Have you completed the task?	☐
2	Is your layout correct?	☐
3	Do you have all the correct information?	☐
4	Is it ordered in the best way?	☐
5	Is the language appropriate for a letter?	☐
6	Have you checked spelling, grammar and punctuation?	☐

Practice 5

You work in the Complaints Department of Ashill Food Products plc of Unit 5, Wolsey Estate, Ashill, Somerset, TN5 8DG. One day you receive the following letter, annotated by your Supervisor.

Last Saturday I bought a packet of your fruit pies at Wateron's in Bridgwater. After I got the packet home I noticed it was all in tatters and the first pies were dented and broken. I thought of writing to the Environmental Health people they were so bad but in the end thought I should contact you direct.

I should be grateful if you would replace my lost pies. I enclose the packet as proof of purchase.

Yours sincerely

Angela Murray

Angela Murray (Miss)

You muse: Not really our problem if the stock was held so long. Angela Murray - name rings a bell - she's complained several times - probably saves old cartons or something.

Write a letter on behalf of your Supervisor, in response to Miss Murray's complaint. Miss Murray lives at 36 Langport Road, Zoyland, Bridgwater, Somerset, TN15 9VX.

(Series 3, 1991, Q1)

Stage 1: Identify the Task

Write a letter on behalf of your Supervisor.

Stage 2: Layout

- your address - Complaints Department, Ashill Food Products plc, Unit 5, Wolsey Estate, Ashill, Somerset, TN5 8DG
- addressee - Miss Murray, 36 Langport Road, Zoyland, Bridgwater, Somerset, TN15 9VX
- date - (today's date)
- salutation - Dear Miss Murray
- subject line - Damaged fruit pies
- close - Yours sincerely
- signature - pp your signature
  name - (Supervisor's name)
  position - Supervisor
  Complaints Department

Now complete the following stages.

Stage 3:   Identify Relevant Information

....
....
....
....
....
....
....
....
....
....
....
....
....
....
....
....
....
....

Stage 4:   Group/Order Relevant Information

....
....
....
....
....
....
....
....
....
....
....
....
....
....
....
....
....
....
....

Stage 5:   Write the Letter

Stage 6:   Check your Work

Checklist: Letter

1   Have you completed the task?
2   Is your layout correct?
3   Do you have all the correct information?
4   Is it ordered in the best way?
5   Is the language appropriate for a letter?
6   Have you checked spelling, grammar and punctuation?

SECTION 1

Practice 6

You are an Accounts Manager for a large engineering company, MacDonald Component Parts Ltd of Halesowen, Birmingham, B9 5PQ.

You receive a letter from G Saunders, the Company Secretary of Parker Brown Ltd of 5 Dukinfield Square, Manchester, M3 2JY which includes the following comment.

> Regret unable to pay your latest bill at present. Can you allow us a little more time? Two major customers having problems themselves. Would also appreciate 3,000 pounds extra credit until difficulties pass. Would further point out that your products not quite up to usual standard.

You are amazed by this and show it to your MD for his comments.

> They've been a little slow in paying before haven't they? Why should we allow them more time? If they're going down, they might drag us down with them. Don't allow them extra credit. Oh, and allow them an extra two months for the current bill - definitely no more after that. Pure cheek to ask for so much extra credit; and even more so to say products are not so good as they have been. Mark my words, they're on their way out.

Write the letter on behalf of MacDonald to be sent in reply to Parker Brown Ltd.

(Series 1, 1992, Q1)

Stage 1: Identify the Task

Write a letter on behalf of MacDonald Component Parts Ltd.

Now complete the following stages.

Stage 2: Layout

your address ....

addressee ....

date ....

salutation ....

subject line ....

close ....

signature/name/position ....

Stage 3:   Identify Relevant Information

....
....
....
....
....
....
....
....
....
....
....
....
....
....
....
....
....
....

Stage 4:   Group/Order Relevant Information

....
....
....
....
....
....
....
....
....
....
....
....
....
....
....
....
....
....

Stage 5: Write the Letter

Stage 6: Check your Work ☑

Checklist: Letter

1	Have you completed the task?	☐
2	Is your layout correct?	☐
3	Do you have all the correct information?	☐
4	Is it ordered in the best way?	☐
5	Is the language appropriate for a letter?	☐
6	Have you checked spelling, grammar and punctuation?	☐

Practice 7

"New Sounds" is a musical company which makes records and compact discs. It is located at Unit 4, Shelton Industrial Estate, Holbarn, Manchester, M60 1AZ. As the Marketing Manager you receive a garbled telephone message from the owner of a large music shop in Dublin, Eire. Apparently the consignment of records he has just received is not the one he ordered. You check the records of the transaction against the message you received.

Shop owner's message:

Ordered 200 sets phase four "New Moon" - received 100 sets phase two "New Horizons".
Ordered 100 sets Neil Diamond "Night at the Greek" - received 100 sets "How to Speak Greek".
Not the first time your communication is at fault. May take business elsewhere. Urgent action required. Please advise immediately.

You telephone the shop owner to say you will investigate straight away, which results in the following note from your despatch clerk.

100 sets of each record "New Moon" and "Night at the Greek" ordered. Despatch of orders correct.
Ref: ARD/103 dated 03/04/91.
Possible mix up with shops or with delivery service.
Will send correct records immediately and arrange collection of unwanted records.

Write the letter to shop owner, Mr S Murphy of O'Connell's Records, 97 Liffey Road, Dublin 9. Use the information above to indicate your continued investigation of a possible, but unusual, delivery error. Give suitable apologies and assurances of future good service.

(Series 2, 1991, Q1)

Now complete the following stages.

Stage 1: Identify the Task

....

Stage 2: Layout

your address ....

addressee ....

date ....

salutation ....

subject line ....

close ....

signature/name/position ....

Stage 3: Identify Relevant Information

....
....
....
....
....
....
....
....
....
....
....
....
....
....
....
....
....
....

Stage 4: Group/Order Relevant Information

....
....
....
....
....
....
....
....
....
....
....
....
....
....
....
....
....
....

Stage 5: Write the Letter

Stage 6: Check your Work

Checklist: Letter

1	Have you completed the task?	☐
2	Is your layout correct?	☐
3	Do you have all the correct information?	☐
4	Is it ordered in the best way?	☐
5	Is the language appropriate for a letter?	☐
6	Have you checked spelling, grammar and punctuation?	☐

Practice 8

You work as Assistant Manager of Planet Travel Ltd of The Green, New Malden, Surrey, KT14 5SU. One day you receive a letter from one of the salesmen of a business in your area which frequently uses your firm. The salesman is very unhappy about arrangements made for a recent trip through southern Europe. You check with the clerk who organised the trip.

Salesman's complaint:

Airport time for four flights was incorrect. Does your clerk know his job?

Hotels were very uncomfortable - I was not expected in two places - food dreadful. Air control strike in Greece - why no mention of this? Several other delays. Not your usual standard of service. Businessmen are blamed for losing trade but are not helped by poor travel data.

Planet Travel Clerk's Response

Sorry, some flight times could not be confirmed. I had a lot to do on the day arranged. Hotels were the ones always used. I did telex places. I cannot do much about food. I don't know a great deal about the rest - sorry!

You warn the clerk that he must take more care. You then send a conciliatory letter to the client Mr N Heilbrunn, Moreway Plastics Ltd, Strangeways Place, Sutton, SU23 1JK.

(Series 4, 1991, Q1)

Write the appropriate letter.

Now complete the following stages.

Stage 1: Identify the Task

....

Stage 2: Layout

your address ....

addressee ....

date ....

salutation ....

subject line ....

close ....

signature/name/position ....

Stage 3: Identify Relevant Information

....
....
....
....
....
....
....
....
....
....
....
....
....
....
....
....
....
....

Stage 4: Group/Order Relevant Information

....
....
....
....
....
....
....
....
....
....
....
....
....
....
....
....
....

Stage 5: Write the Letter

Stage 6: Check your Work ☑

Checklist: Letter

1	Have you completed the task?	☐
2	Is your layout correct?	☐
3	Do you have all the correct information?	☐
4	Is it ordered in the best way?	☐
5	Is the language appropriate for a letter?	☐
6	Have you checked spelling, grammar and punctuation?	☐

Practice 9

John Williams is not a happy man. The antiques dealer from 17 The High Street, North Walsham, NR3 5AJ is annoyed with British Rail. He has just experienced a number of difficulties travelling to Bristol via London from his home in Norfolk. The Station Master's representative at London's Waterloo Station is both amused and annoyed to get a letter from John Williams. The essence of John Williams's letter is:

> Told the wrong information at my local BR office - missed train for Norwich from North Walsham by three minutes. Trains normally seem to be late - I didn't think one would be early for a change. No catering facilities open at North Walsham. When I got to Norwich I found I'd missed the London express - again no meal facilities on a slow train to Liverpool Street. Mis-directed to the wrong terminus for Bristol. Sent to Euston instead of Paddington by a very young know-it-all at Liverpool Street - thought there was something wrong. All these delays forced me to spend an extra night in Bristol - very expensive as things turned out - the bill for the extra night is enclosed.

"If he'd travelled at all, he must know where to change in London", said the representative at Waterloo. "He should also know he has written to the wrong office. His problems are with Anglian region of British Rail, not with Network South East. How did he come to choose this address? He must also know that if he does not turn up on time, he may miss the train. Timetables are normally adhered to. He should certainly know about catering arrangements. They're always listed on timetables. He should know his own stations facilities better than us; we're such a distance away! Anyway, I suppose we'd better point out gently to him the fact that he has written to the wrong office and tell him to address his problem to BR, Anglia Region, Norwich, and that we decline to pay his bill!"

Write the letter from the Station Master's Representative at Waterloo Station, London, SE1 to John Williams.

(Series 3, 1993, Q1)

Now complete the following stages.

Stage 1:   Identify the Task

....

Stage 2:   Layout

your address ....

addressee ....

date ....

salutation ....

subject line ....

close ....

signature/name/position ....

Stage 3: Identify Relevant Information

....

....

....

....

....

....

....

....

....

....

....

....

....

....

....

....

....

....

Stage 4: Group/Order Relevant Information

....

....

....

....

....

....

....

....

....

....

....

....

....

....

....

....

....

....

Stage 5: Write the Letter

Stage 6: Check your Work ☑

Checklist: Letter

1	Have you completed the task?	☐
2	Is your layout correct?	☐
3	Do you have all the correct information?	☐
4	Is it ordered in the best way?	☐
5	Is the language appropriate for a letter?	☐
6	Have you checked spelling, grammar and punctuation?	☐

Practice 10

A Cinema Manager at South Cheriton in Kent is very upset. His management of a three cinema complex in the High Street of the Kentish town depends very much upon the cooperation and efficiency of the distributors who supply him with the films he shows. In the past he has suffered minor problems at the last minute. But it seems that the van bringing the replacement films this time is two days overdue - almost unheard of in the local cinema trade.

If the films are overdue, Fred Jones, the Cinema Manager has three alternatives:

- Close the Cinema.
- Hold on to the films currently showing and show them for extra days (with consequences for the cinemas next in line).
- Show back up films that he has in store.

Unfortunately: Money is also tied up in advertising (he will have paid in advance to advertise for films that are no longer available - and he could even be open to some form of legal action).

He could lose cinema clients.

He couldn't afford to close the cinema.

If he showed the films for extra days, he wouldn't make any more money (most people who wanted to see the film would have seen it at the advertised times).

If he showed the back up films, the reputation of the cinema could plummet.

On the third day, the Cinema Manager learns from the distributors that the films should be delivered in two days time - apparently an influenza bug has severely upset schedules for delivery. However, the Cinema Manager feels that the distributors should have more effective 'fail-safe' systems of delivery and intends to tell the distributors in writing about the impact of the non delivery of films.

Write Fred Jones' letter from The Kent Film Complex, High Street, South Cheriton, CT13 7AJ, to the film distributors - GB Eurofilm Company, Wardour Street, London, SW12 4AJ

(Series 2, 1993, Q1)

Now complete the following stages.

Stage 1: Identify the Task

....

Stage 2: Layout

your address ....

addressee ....

date ....

salutation ....

subject line ....

close ....

signature/name/position ....

Stage 3:   Identify Relevant Information

....
....
....
....
....
....
....
....
....
....
....
....
....
....
....
....
....
....
....

Stage 4:   Group/Order Relevant Information

....
....
....
....
....
....
....
....
....
....
....
....
....
....
....
....
....
....

Stage 5: Write the Letter

Stage 6: Check your Work ☑

Checklist: Letter

1 Have you completed the task? ☐
2 Is your layout correct? ☐
3 Do you have all the correct information? ☐
4 Is it ordered in the best way? ☐
5 Is the language appropriate for a letter? ☐
6 Have you checked spelling, grammar and punctuation? ☐

SECTION 2:   Reports

Introduction

The report always appears in Question 2.

Stage 1:   Identify the Task

Read the question and work out exactly what you are required to do. The instruction at the bottom normally reads "Write the report" or "Complete the report" or "Submit the report".

Stage 2:   Layout

At this level there are various possibilities. The most common layout for a general report includes the following:

To:
From:
Date:
Subject:
Findings:
Recommendations:

A useful alternative for reports requiring a for and against argument is:

To:
From:
Date:
Subject:
The Case For:
The Case Against:
Recommendations:

According to the Chief Examiner, "The layout is determined by the purpose of the report and the nature of the information..."

Stage 3:   Identify Relevant Information

A report is usually asked for and requires details of what you found out, how you found it out and your recommendations. It is normally very factual as all information in it must be relevant to the subject heading.

Stage 4:   Group/Order Relevant Information

The information in the question is sometimes presented in a suitable order. Often, however, information is mixed up or repeated. After you have identified the relevant information make sure it is grouped so that points are presented in a logical order.

Stage 5:   Write the Report

Reports are matter-of-fact and to the point. Language is therefore neutral and factual. Numbering points is a useful technique.

Stage 6:   Check your Work

Check List: Report

The following is a list of points to check when you write a report.

1   Have you completed the task?
2   Is the layout you have chosen appropriate to the task?
3   Is the information relevant?
4   Is the information in the right order?
5   Is the language appropriate?
6   Have you given some recommendations?
7   Have you checked spelling, grammar and punctuation?

SECTION 2

Practice 1

Problems seem to be mounting for the Director of Environmental Health and Cleansing Services of the Borough of Gillingsworth. Following complaints about lack of cleanliness in the borough by comment in the local press, the Director has been asked to prepare a report on Rubbish Collection in the borough.

Using the following information, write his report for the Environmental Health Committee.

(Series 1, 1993, Q2)

Lack of funds over the years has meant that important equipment has not been replaced. Several severe winters have caused us to spend more and more money.
(Deputy Director)

Last year, 15 staff left the cleansing services section - only 4 have been replaced.
(Personnel)

Suspected outbreak of Typhoid in Gillingsworth. Town on 'Red Alert'.
Daily Brief

We've introduced 200 new waste bins but these have largely been ignored by the public.
(Cleansing Operatives)

Industrial concerns and large users do not encourage good practice. The local river is full of chemical effluent.

Statistics
Each year 58,000 tonnes of rubbish are collected in the borough.
Each month 10,000 bulk containers are emptied.
Each week 53,000 dustbins are emptied.
Each week 1,000 tonnes of civic amenity rubbish are collected.

The Spring "hurricane" caused considerable damage - the borough has not recovered from that.

"Privatise public cleansing in the borough".
(leader in the Gillingsworth Gleaner)

What wee need is a local awareness campaign for a tidier borough.
(Teachers' Group)

We have tried to encourage school children to be tidier but it's a losing battle. It all begins at home.
(Health Education Officer)

"Total confidence in heath officials after rat scare".
(Gillingsworth Gleaner)

Borough wines Green prize; triumph for Cleansing Director.

Plans exist for wide scale environmental improvements - only the money is needed.
(Town Hall Official)

"Cleanliness is an education issue. It is imperative that rubbish collection remains in local government hands and that it merits greater public investment."
(Local Unions)

Less rubbish would bring more visitors.
(Local Tourist Office)

Are we worse than other areas?
(Pensioners' Groups)

Stage 1: Identify the Task

Write a report.

Stage 2: Layout

To: Director of Environmental Health and Cleansing Services
From: (your name)
Date: (today's date)
Subject: Rubbish Collection in the Borough

Appropriate headings for this task are: Introduction, Findings, Recommendations.

Stage 3: Identify Relevant Information

-   rubbish collection in the borough
-   no money to replace equipment
-   bad weather caused extra spending
-   not all staff who left have been replaced
-   importance of press to influence opinion
-   200 bins bought but not used by the public
-   large users don't follow good practice of waste disposal
-   statistics: 58,000 tonnes of rubbish collected annually
                1,000 tonnes of rubbish collected weekly
                10,000 bulk containers emptied monthly
                53,000 dustbins emptied weekly
-   more money should be available for public cleansing
-   less rubbish would bring more visitors
-   asked staff for comments
-   asked representatives of local committees
-   checked newspaper articles
-   analysed statistics

Stage 4: Group/Order Relevant Information

Subject: Rubbish Collection in the Borough

Introduction: Report for the Environmental Health Committee about rubbish collection in the borough.

Findings: 1   Funding has been cut: a) equipment has not been replaced.
                                                    b) staff who left have not all been replaced.
                        2   Money spent on bins/not used by the public.
                        3   Individuals/companies do not have good practice of waste disposal.
                        4   Problem of bad weather.
                        5   Influence of press - positive and negative.
                        6   Statistics: 58,000 tonnes of rubbish collected annually.
                            1,000 tonnes of civic amenity rubbish collected weekly
                            10,000 bulk containers emptied monthly
                            53,000 dustbins emptied weekly
                        7   Representatives of local committees say more money should be available for public cleansing/to keep borough tidy.

Recommendations: 1   Budget for awareness groups/activities/advertising/information evenings.
                        2   Look into recycling possibilities.
                        3   Review plans.

Stage 5:   Write the Report

To: Director of Environmental Health and Cleansing Services
From: (your name)
Date: (today's date)
Subject: Rubbish Collection in the Borough

Introduction:

The Director of Environmental Health and Cleansing Services has asked me to prepare a report on rubbish collection in the borough for the Environmental Health Committee. I have questioned staff, analysed statistics, collected newspaper articles and spoken to representatives of various local committees.

Findings:

1   Funding has been cut over the past few years. This has meant that:
     a) equipment has not been replaced.
     b) staff who left have not all been replaced.

2   Money has been spent on 200 new bins which are not used by the public.

3   Individuals as well as companies are not aware of environmental problems and do not follow good practice of waste disposal.

4   Bad weather over the past few years has caused major damage and extra cost.

5   The press can influence public opinion both positively and negatively.

6   Statistics for the borough are at present: 58,000 tonnes of rubbish collected annually
                                                 1,000 tonnes of civic amenity rubbish collected weekly
                                                 10,000 bulk containers emptied monthly
                                                 53,000 dustbins emptied weekly

7   Representatives of local committees believe more money should be available for keeping the borough tidy, and on no account should public cleansing be privatised.

Recommendations:

1   A Budget should be made available for:
     a   setting up awareness groups.
     b   advertising campaign in newspapers.
     c   organising information evenings.

2   Plans for environmental improvements should be reviewed to make sure that money is being spent in the best way.

3   Recycling possibilities should be introduced eg bottle banks, old paper collections. These should have clear instructions, be in useful locations and coincide with advertising.

Stage 6: Check your Work   ☑

Checklist: Report

1   Have you completed the task?   ☑
2   Is the layout you have chosen appropriate for the task?   ☑
3   Is the information relevant?   ☑
4   Is the information in the right order?   ☑
5   Is the language appropriate?   ☑
6   Have you given some recommendations?   ☑
7   Have you checked spelling, grammar and punctuation?   ☑

Practice 2

Murrays Bank of Ullacross in the Highlands of Scotland is in a town of 15,000 people - but its hinterland covers 55,000 inhabitants. It has never had foreign exchange facilities. Those wanting foreign currency have to make arrangements several weeks in advance to get currency sent from the headquarters of the bank in Edinburgh - or else they trek to Inverness forty miles away.

Faced with increasing pressure from local businesses, your manager asks you - his "troubleshooter" - to investigate the "pros and cons" of establishing a "Foreign Department".

You compile a report based on the following information from a cross-section of the community.

(Series 4, 1992, Q2)

Allen's Papermills

Facility greatly needed.
Exchange is so volatile - waiting
days can cost a fortune.

Rough Poll of Consumers

Foreign Department is a good idea	43%
Not essential	47%
Would help business	35%
(10% undecided)	
Would help non business consumers	15%
Help holidaymakers generally	52%

Questions Raised by Consumers

Just for a trial period?
Suppose it would cost the bank money?
How much would it cost us?
How much standard charges, commission, etc?
Which currencies would it stock?
Foreign currency accounts available?

Alan Mackie, Tenant Farmer

Go abroad? Never! Don't need foreign currency.
Facility would cost me money!

Rotary Club

Would a self service facility - as on
the continent - not please people?

Jane Frobisher, School Teacher

We need it. Such a hassle otherwise.
You try to organise school trips - even to Norway.
Every bank needs it.

Reverend MacAllan

Useful addition to bank's services.

Local Business in Ullacross itself

Lewis, Stationer	Needed. Great many foreign magazines these days. Many tourists too - like to read news from abroad.
Andrews, Florist	Sometimes useful - for Euro connections.
Munday, Architect	Very necessary. Very surprised not available before.
McAfie, "Scottish Foods"	Not much call really but nice to know it's there. Doubt if more than 2% of my customers need it.

SECTION 2

Stage 1: Identify the Task

Compile a report.

Stage 2: Layout

To: The Manager, Murrays Bank
From: (your name)
Date: (today's date)
Subject: Provision of Foreign Exchange Department - "pros and cons"

Appropriate headings for this task are: Introduction, The case for, The case against, Recommendations.

Stage 3: Identify Relevant Information

- establish "pros and cons" of establishing a "Foreign Department"
- Ullacross population
- hinterland
- arrangements weeks in advance
- Inverness
- pressure from local businessmen
- exchange so volatile, risks for businesses
- facility will cost all customers
- organise school trips - made easier
- useful addition to services
- poll results
- questions raised by customers
- local shop owners' opinions

Stage 4: Group/Order Relevant Information

Subject: Provision of "Foreign Department" - "pros and cons"
Introduction: Report for Manager, Murrays Bank, on feasibility of establishing Foreign Exchange Department in Ullacross.

The case for:

1   Ullacross population 15,000.
2   Hinterland 55,000.
3   Never had foreign exchange facilities.
4   At present arrange exchange weeks in advance.
5   Or travel to banks in Inverness.
6   Pressure from local businessmen.
7   Exchange so volatile, risky for business.
8   Local shop owners in favour.
9   Useful addition to services.
10   Help for organising trips abroad.
11   Poll 43% in favour.

The case against:

1   Facility will cost all bank account holders.
2   Poll 47% not essential.
3   Poll 55% wouldn't help business.
4   Poll 85% of no help to non-business community.

Recommendations: 1   Introduce facilities.
                   2   Need public relations work.
                   3   Trial period in summer.
                   4   Keep costs down.
                   5   Reasons: a) Would be useful addition.
                                 b) Competitors not offering this service.

Stage 5: Write the Report

To:	The Manager, Murrays Bank
From:	(your name)
Date:	(today's date)
Subject:	"Provision of Foreign Department" - "pros and cons"

Introduction:

Following the request to investigate the feasibility of establishing a Foreign Exchange facility in Ullacross, I have questioned locals and local businessmen and compiled a poll of consumers' opinions.

The case for:

1 Ullacross, with a population of 15,000, and a hinterland of a further 55,000, has never had any foreign exchange facilities.

2 At present currency has to be ordered several weeks in advance or customers have to go to Inverness.

3 The local business community is pressurising for this facility to be made available.

4 Exchange rates are so volatile and having to wait days can cost firms dearly.

5 Local shop owners are in favour and the general opinion is it would be a useful addition to the bank's services.

6 This would be a help for residents organising trips abroad and also for foreign tourists in the town.

7 A rough poll of consumers showed 43% were in favour and 52% thought it would help holidaymakers in the area.

The case against:

1 The general concern voiced was that the facility would cost the bank money and therefore ultimately all bank account holders would have to pay for it.

2 The question most asked was, "How much will it cost?"

3 Rough poll of consumers showed 47% considered it not essential, 55% were of the opinion it would be of no help to business and a staggering 85% didn't think it would help the non-business community either.

Recommendations:

The facility should be introduced, although a certain amount of public relations work will be needed to show the usefulness of this facility. It would be best to introduce it for a trial period in the summer months and to keep the costs as low as possible.

Reasons:

1 It would be a useful addition to the bank's services.
2 Competitors are not offering the service at the moment.
3 The business community and local traders are very much in favour.

Now complete the following stage

Stage 6: Check your Work

Checklist: Report

1	Have you completed the task?	☐
2	Is the layout you have chosen appropriate for the task?	☐
3	Is the information relevant?	☐
4	Is the information in the right order?	☐
5	Is the language appropriate?	☐
6	Have you given some recommendations?	☐
7	Have you checked spelling, grammar and punctuation?	☐

SECTION 2

Practice 3

"I'd like to change the function of that spare room we've got", said the Group Personnel Manager of a large consultancy firm to his chief assistant one day. "The room is not really appropriate as an interviewing room. I think there is a much greater need to establish a library for employees - especially those who are students of one kind or another. Shelving and other materials can be obtained from other rooms in the building or from stores. Could you prepare a report on the practical aspects of converting the room and include a feasibility study on its potential use?"

As the Personnel Manager's Assistant, write the report, using the material below.

(Series 3, 1992, Q2)

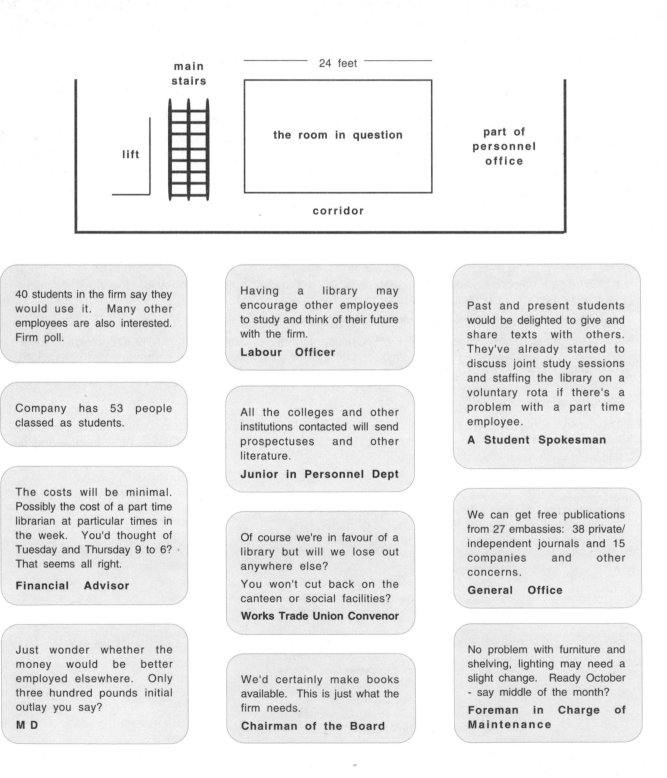

40 students in the firm say they would use it. Many other employees are also interested. Firm poll.

Having a library may encourage other employees to study and think of their future with the firm.
Labour Officer

Past and present students would be delighted to give and share texts with others. They've already started to discuss joint study sessions and staffing the library on a voluntary rota if there's a problem with a part time employee.
A Student Spokesman

Company has 53 people classed as students.

All the colleges and other institutions contacted will send prospectuses and other literature.
Junior in Personnel Dept

The costs will be minimal. Possibly the cost of a part time librarian at particular times in the week. You'd thought of Tuesday and Thursday 9 to 6? That seems all right.
Financial Advisor

Of course we're in favour of a library but will we lose out anywhere else?
You won't cut back on the canteen or social facilities?
Works Trade Union Convenor

We can get free publications from 27 embassies: 38 private/ independent journals and 15 companies and other concerns.
General Office

Just wonder whether the money would be better employed elsewhere. Only three hundred pounds initial outlay you say?
M D

We'd certainly make books available. This is just what the firm needs.
Chairman of the Board

No problem with furniture and shelving, lighting may need a slight change. Ready October - say middle of the month?
Foreman in Charge of Maintenance

Stage 1: Identify the Task

Write the report.

Stage 2: Layout

To: The Group Personnel Manager
From: (your name), Personnel Manager's Assistant
Date: (today's date)
Subject: Room Conversion

Appropriate headings for this task are: Introduction, Findings, Recommendations.

Stage 3: Identify Relevant Information

- feasibility study on potential use for spare room
- practical aspects of converting the room
- not appropriate as interview room
- need to establish library for employees
- shelving available from other rooms
- 53 people in company are students
- 40 students would use it
- other employees would also be interested
- we can get materials from colleges and institutions
- lighting may need to be changed
- minimal costs, possible part-time staff
- £300 initial outlay could be better used (MD)
- books available (Chairman of the Board)
- will other facilities be cut?
- free publications from 27 embassies, 38 journals, 15 companies etc
- encourage others to study

Stage 4: Group/Order Relevant Information

Subject: Room Conversion

Introduction: Report for Group Personnel Manager on the feasibility of converting spare room into a library.

Findings:
- 53 people in company are students
- 40 would use the facility
- other employees are also interested
- others will be encouraged to study
- shelving available from other rooms/stores
- employees are prepared to staff the room themselves
- books provided by the Chairman
- other free publications provided by 27 embassies, 38 journals, 15 companies, etc.
- minimal cost (£300 initial outlay)
- £300 could be spent elsewhere
- staff are worried they will lose other facilities
- lighting may have to be changed

Recommendations: Convert room into library but reassure staff they will not lose other facilities.

Reasons:
a   Room no good as interview room, therefore is not used.
b   Cost of conversion would be minimal.
c   Interest among staff is high and need is there.
d   Staff could qualify themselves further.

SECTION 2

Now complete the following stages.

Stage 5: Write the Report

Stage 6: Check your Work

Checklist: Report

1	Have you completed the task?	☐
2	Is the layout you have chosen appropriate for the task?	☐
3	Is the information relevant?	☐
4	Is the information in the right order?	☐
5	Is the language appropriate?	☐
6	Have you given some recommendations?	☐
7	Have you checked spelling, grammar and punctuation?	☐

Practice 4

Mr Eric Knowles, Managing Director of Teesdale Chemicals plc - a firm which is sited on the side of a major river, the River Brent, is a worried man. He has just been informed by one of his Personal Assistants that the firm is currently discharging dangerous waste into the river. Normally the firm discharges certain elements into the river, but these are strictly controlled by the firm and by the local river and waste authority. Mr. Knowles asks you, as the Personal Assistant, to let him have a report on the problem as soon as possible - 4.30 pm that day at the latest - indicating areas of greatest concern and action necessary.

You use the material below.

(Series 2, 1992, Q2)

Notes you have made:
Estimate 153,000 gallons of toxic materials already in river.
Cause of problem faulty secondary pipe taking waste from transport area - pipe fractured in several places.

Action taken so far:
Transport section ceased functioning as a work unit. All pumping of waste there halted. Experts looking at pump.

It'll cost at least 2 million pounds to contain the problem + the cost of lost production + cost of wages, extra staff, materials + possible law suits, etc.

Suggest you warn the MD and Board to set aside 5 million pounds to cover exigencies. Let's hope no person dies or serious epidemic ensues.

Firm's Chief Accountant

Conservancy Board (phones to firm)

"Stop emission of waste. Thousands of fish already dead. Peril/hazard for all wildlife on the river. Require massive emergency help."

Teesmouth Borough and their Fishermen's Cooperatives now worried about danger to fish in the sea at the mouth of the river.

Radio

Greenpeace - "On our way. Stop process of waste disposal."

Messages
Various newspapers and radio stations phoned - most sending reporters.

"I wish it had never happened. We were told of pipe stresses yesterday and were planning to reinforce the pipe today."
Firm's Maintenance Engineer

Note from Personnel
I see nothing for it but to halt production completely.
Lay off non essential staff for a week.

Message Received
Brent Rivers Authority sending experts and observers for urgent talks.

Stage 1: Identify the Task

Write a report.

Stage 2: Layout

To: Mr Eric Knowles MD
From: (your name), Personal Assistant
Date: (today's date)
Subject: Accidental discharging of waste into the River Brent

Appropriate headings for this task are: Introduction, Findings, Recommendations.

Stage 3: Identify Relevant Information

- firm discharging dangerous waste into the River Brent
- areas of greatest concern
- action necessary
- situation at present
- cause
- action taken so far

Now complete the following stages.

Stage 4: Group/Order Relevant Information

....

....

....

....

....

....

....

....

....

....

....

....

....

....

Stage 5: Write the Report

Stage 6: Check your Work ✓

Checklist: Report

1	Have you completed the task?	☐
2	Is the layout you have chosen appropriate for the task?	☐
3	Is the information relevant?	☐
4	Is the information in the right order?	☐
5	Is the language appropriate?	☐
6	Have you given some recommendations?	☐
7	Have you checked spelling, grammar and punctuation?	☐

Practice 5

"I think we'll have to develop new training strategies. We don't seem to be able to keep the youngsters we get - our competitors offer more to them. See if you can produce a report for the next meeting of the Personnel Committee. See what people think about training. Your recommendations would be valuable," says the Managing Director of a large firm of arms manufacturers in Birmingham to you, a Senior Administrative Officer in the Personnel Department.

Write the report using the comments below.

(Series 1, 1992, Q2)

It isn't just the training - it's the lack of opportunity afterwards.

A Skilled Worker

Personnel Statistics

One third of our ordinary trainees leave over two years - and most of our apprentices express a wish to leave. When they're qualified, about half go elsewhere - mostly to Forgans.

"Because the firm was doing badly, I lost my day release. What kind of deal is that?"

Disgruntled Apprentice

It's not quite what I thought it would be - everything's so boring after a while./

Second Year Trainee

We need to offer our skilled men more and make training more purposeful

Training Officer

I like being here. The lads are friendly. I know I'd get more elsewhere - but they demand more of you too.

Can we reduce the length of traineeships and apprenticeships by at least a year - and fix more tempting wages and salaries?

(A question you ask of Finance)

Nobody seems to know what they're doing in training. If you do become a skilled man, you're just a glorified machinist.

Skilled Worker of Ten Years

The Works Foreman says, "It seems we train people. When they're qualified, they go to Forgans for higher wages."

Surprisingly 78% of staff say they wouldn't move.

R & D

Here I'm paid two hundred and sixty pounds a week. At Patterson's I'd get twenty pounds more - and they don't pay such good money either. Forgans - now they pay real money; three hundred pounds for my skills.

"Our work quality is good but Forgans impress buyers with their aggressiveness.":

Assistant Sales Director

Stage 1: Identify the Task

Write the report.

Stage 2: Layout

To: The Personnel Committee
From: (your name), Senior Administrative Officer
Date: (today's date)
Subject: Staff Training

Appropriate headings for this task are: Introduction, Findings, Recommendations.

Now complete the following stages.

Stage 3: Identify Relevant Information

....
....
....
....
....
....
....
....
....
....
....
....

Stage 4: Group/Order Relevant Information

....
....
....
....
....
....
....
....
....
....
....
....

Stage 5:   Write the Report

Stage 6:   Check your Work

Checklist: Report

1	Have you completed the task?	☐
2	Is the layout you have chosen appropriate for the task?	☐
3	Is the information relevant?	☐
4	Is the information in the right order?	☐
5	Is the language appropriate?	☐
6	Have you given some recommendations?	☐
7	Have you checked spelling, grammar and punctuation?	☐

Practice 6

The Managing Director of a food packaging firm has expansion problems. He tells his Personal Assistant "I'm sorry, there's nothing for it. Because of expansion we'll have to take over the firm's social club premises. We cannot afford land in the vicinity and that which we can afford is too far away. Two sites would cripple the firm." Then, after some thought, he says, "You'd better prepare a feasibility study - have a chat with the work force to see if they'd truly object. Let me have their and your recommendations in the report."

As the MD's Personal Assistant you consider the following:

Production Shop Floor

Diabolical liberty! They never go there. What about our darts?

We relax after lunch. Where else can we go?

Can they give us something else instead?

Numbers? About 150 (of 250 workers) have used this place in the last few weeks.

Senior Staff

No loss - we never go near it. Alternatives? Why?

Personnel

We want success - but at this price? The shop floor won't like it. A "quid pro quo" will be needed. Alternatively, something else to appease the shop floor.

Clerical Staff

It's a shame really. We know that the shop floor really love that club. They'll want something, that's for sure. Us? We never use it. Prefer the wine bar around the corner. Mind you, we'd go if it was improved. Perhaps the boss could provide a better place for all of us.

Trade Union Reps

Isn't it marvellous? The workers succeed and then they have to suffer. We'll take a poll on what the workers think.

Trade Union Poll

Against the firm's expansion into the social club	89%
For the firm's expansion if alternative premises are found locally	59%
Think the firm should provide other compensation	78%
Would like social club a few miles away	7%

TU Verdict

The management will have to consider issues carefully. This could lead to direct confrontation - despite the success of the firm

Extracts from the MD's Circular Letter to Staff

"... in the interest of further profitable expansion it will benefit all staff shortly... guarantee of work and then new facilities can be developed... I hope you all agree it will then bring greater prosperity. I look forward to a happy future for all of us."

Now write the appropriate report using the above information

(Series 4, 1991, Q2)

Stage 1: Identify the Task

Write the appropriate report.

Now complete the following stages.

Stage 2: Layout

To: ....

From: ....

Date: ....

Subject: ....

Appropriate headings for this task are: ....

Stage 3: Identify Relevant Information

....

....

....

....

....

....

....

....

....

....

....

....

Stage 4: Group/Order Relevant Information

....

....

....

....

....

....

....

....

....

....

....

Stage 5: Write the Report

Stage 6: Check your Work ✓

Checklist: Report

1	Have you completed the task?	☐
2	Is the layout you have chosen appropriate for the task?	☐
3	Is the information relevant?	☐
4	Is the information in the right order?	☐
5	Is the language appropriate?	☐
6	Have you given some recommendations?	☐
7	Have you checked spelling, grammar and punctuation?	☐

Practice 7

"I'm really appalled", said the Managing Director of an exporting firm. "Here we are just a while away from 1992 and how many of our staff know anything about Europe - let alone the rest of the world? I think now is the time to inform our staff about EC initiatives affecting this firm. Don't they know that Brussels determine the future of this organisation? Submit an initial report, call it 'Staff Knowledge of the EC'. Let me know if you think they know anything. Best to ask in three categories: the younger staff, older staff and senior staff."

Your circulate a staff questionnaire. Here are some of the main responses.

Now write the report using the information below.

(Series 3, 1991, Q2)

Do you know what the EC stands for?
43% **all staff** 'Yes'; 57% 'No'.

Of the 43% who answered 'Yes'; do you know
what the EC does?   30% - Yes
                     70% - No

Young Office Staff

Where is the EC Commission located?
30%   Paris
30%   Brussels
10%   Bonn
25%   London
5%   Berlin

How many countries are in the EC?
5%   Twelve
33%   Nine
17%   Eight
13%   Six
32%   no idea

How important is the EC?

No importance.   Place for civil servants.
Employment for a few. We don't have to do
what they think. We need to trade with them but
that's all.

Older Staff

Do you: feel you know about the EC   35%
         feel EC is important   38%
         feel EC is unimportant   52%

Are you uncertain - no real views? 10%

Could it affect your jobs?   35% Yes

Are you aware of any
significant EC activities?   35% Yes

Do you think about the EC
in your everyday lives?   35% Yes

80% senior staff feel EC is important (65% feel
it is important every day).

20% senior staff feel EC is overstated in its
every day significance.

"I like Europe for holidays. Also I've spent a
year in Munich. I feel European and the EC is
a good thing, but the media don't treat it as
important."

"I've travelled more in the USA than in Europe.
I don't really fee European. No, the EC doesn't
really affect me."

"Better publicity would help. I feel that it is very
important, one should experience how
important."

32%   feel EC is important.
23%   feel EC is important in every day life.
18%   feel it could be important for the firm's
      future.

30%   feel that it is important to establish more
      markets worldwide.
23%   feel it is important to expand in Europe.

Now complete the following stages.

Stage 1: Identify the Task

....

Stage 2: Layout

To: ....

From: ....

Date: ....

Subject: ....

Appropriate headings for this task are: ....

Stage 3: Identify Relevant Information

....

....

....

....

....

....

....

....

....

....

....

....

Stage 4: Group/Order Relevant Information

....

....

....

....

....

....

....

....

....

....

....

....

Stage 5:   Write the Report

Stage 6:   Check your Work ☑

Checklist: Report

1	Have you completed the task?	☐
2	Is the layout you have chosen appropriate for the task?	☐
3	Is the information relevant?	☐
4	Is the information in the right order?	☐
5	Is the language appropriate?	☐
6	Have you given some recommendations?	☐
7	Have you checked spelling, grammar and punctuation?	☐

Practice 8

"We must get more tourists to visit the area," said the Tourist Manager for the Arronsay Islands off the coasts of Britain. You, as his assistant, are given the responsibility for getting information on visitors to the islands and suggesting new ways of attracting visitors. You are required to present your information, with recommendations, in the form of a report.

Write the report based on the following information.

(Series 2, 1991, Q2)

Visitors to Arronsay

1980	1985	1986	1988	1989
50,345	61,897	73,048	60,246	51,124

In 1989, of 51,124 visitors:

- 3% were described as business travellers.
- 73% were from the Scottish mainland.
- 17% were from England.
- 6% were from Europe.
- 1% was from the rest of the world.

Holiday preferences of visitors:

1	sun	4	food
2	entertainment	5	sights
3	travel	6	sport

Your fact list of what Arronsay has to offer:

a) islands
b) beaches
c) one cinema and one theatre - both on the main island
d) walks

Problems Affecting Travel to Arronsay

1980	Very bad summer - much rain.
1981	British Rail ferry link strike.
1982	Bad summer.
1983	British Rail strike on mainland.
1984	Bad summer.
1985	£ devalued - British stayed at home.
1986	Dollar under pressure.
1987	Stock market problem. Bad summer. External terrorism.
1988	Ferry strike.
1989	£ under pressure. Transport strikes on mainland, holiday makers prefer holidays in the sun.

Arronsay attitudes to visitors:

"I can take them or leave them..." "Why should I talk to them?" "Our facilities were good enough for my father..." "They're all foreigners."

Your Follow Up Action

a) You decide that Arronsay has little to offer shoppers, beach and sun worshippers, sight seers, but has a lot to offer naturalists and those who like the natural environment, walkers and boating.

b) You consult advertisers and market research organisations in the UK who would be willing to offer guidance.

c) You conduct a survey of Arronsay institutions to see what facilities they offer. You discover there are only a few places to stay - and most of these offer limited bed and breakfast facilities.

d) You decide to ask your superior and the British Tourist Authority for careful development of an accommodation register, communal entertainment facilities, regular boat trips, putting greens, more investment...

e) You consult travel experts who can promise designed packages for visitors (with travel concessions) and appropriate publicity.

f) You consult the British Tourist Authority who can assist Arronsay with publicity - worldwide, finance for projects, ideas for development, audio visual aids and materials assistance, etc.

SECTION 2

Now complete the following stages.

Stage 1: Identify the Task

....

Stage 2: Layout

To: ....

From: ....

Date: ....

Subject: ....

Appropriate headings for this task are: ....

Stage 3: Identify Relevant Information

....

....

....

....

....

....

....

....

....

....

....

....

Stage 4: Group/Order Relevant Information

....

....

....

....

....

....

....

....

....

....

....

....

Stage 5:   Write the Report

Stage 6:   Check your Work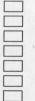

Checklist: Report

1	Have you completed the task?	☐
2	Is the layout you have chosen appropriate for the task?	☐
3	Is the information relevant?	☐
4	Is the information in the right order?	☐
5	Is the language appropriate?	☐
6	Have you given some recommendations?	☐
7	Have you checked spelling, grammar and punctuation?	☐

Practice 9

You are the Assistant Training Manager of Cormorant Airspace of New Weston, Avon. Your Training Manager confides that potential recruits for apprenticeships, when tested recently, performed very badly. He wants you to write a report on the results of the various tests and to recommend strategies. The report will be sent to local schools. All the candidates for these apprenticeships were boys.

(Series 3, 1993, Q2)

Mathematics

12% candidates got all answers right.

33% failed every question.

Graphs - generally incompetent.

18% got them mostly correct.

Oral arithmetic - unbelievable (5% correct).

Communication (English)

Third of candidates good - most appalling.

Spelling weak, grammar almost non existent.

Orally - I wouldn't let any of them near customers.

Mechanical Drawing

Youngsters like this but they don't take care.

Discussion revealed:

Many had knowledge of computers (not tested); some also able to use word processors. Very little knowledge of geography (untested) or history (also untested).

General Manager of Firm

"We are not going to lower our standards for anyone."

Remarks from the Boys

Didn't expect tasks to be so hard; thought we were prepared. I'd make a good trainee - not so good at school subjects - that's all. Can always go back to school. Got another chance at Larrabee's.

Manager of Production Shop

Too many youngsters treat work as a game - but it's deadly serious. The firm needs to work and survive. It cannot do that with a poorly qualified workforce.

Personnel

We'll advertise again and recruit from a wider area. Schools must prepare youngsters more effectively. They must look tidy too.

Comment from those testing:

Not as good as the girls recruited for secretarial positions. Boys lacked maturity and general knowledge.

Girls who had been recruited earlier:

"I think we were better prepared. But we also knew how much school meant. Some of them *(the boys) just wanted to leave school."

Comment from a father employed by the firm as a fitter:

Disappointed. I told him how important it was - but he knows it all! He'll have to try again.

Test Results

Passed all areas	5%
Failed one area	3%
Failed two areas	28%
Failed all areas	64%

Now complete the following stages.

Stage 1:   Identify the Task

....

Stage 2:   Layout

To: ....

From: ....

Date: ....

Subject: ....

Appropriate headings for this task are: ....

Stage 3:   Identify Relevant Information

....
....
....
....
....
....
....
....
....
....
....
....

Stage 4:   Group/Order Relevant Information

....
....
....
....
....
....
....
....
....
....
....
....

Stage 5:   Write the Report

Stage 6:   Check your Work

Checklist: Report

1   Have you completed the task?
2   Is the layout you have chosen appropriate for the task?
3   Is the information relevant?
4   Is the information in the right order?
5   Is the language appropriate?
6   Have you given some recommendations?
7   Have you checked spelling, grammar and punctuation?

Practice 10

"I'm more than a little concerned about the number of accidents we seem to be having in the firm", says the Managing Director to you, his Safety Officer, one day. "A production engineering firm like Lemans should have a better record surely? Could you give me a report on safety in this factory? Within a week if you can - with recommendations."

Write the report, using the information below.

(Series 2, 1993, Q2)

Production Shop Foreman

There have been 30 accidents among 100 employees in a year; piece-work is so monotonous. Married women seem to suffer most.

We've had ten accidents with drivers in the last three months - we always expect them to be trained. We just give them a vehicle!

Despatch Manager

The workers are just not safety conscious. Too many are tired when they come to work, or they eat too much - and then stress takes a hand.

Nurses at the Firm

Well of course, something should be done. There are just too many accidents. I think the firm should institute an inquiry with specialists.

Parent of a Worker

It seems as if people in the office also have higher stress related illnesses than elsewhere. Is it unsuitable building syndrome?

Hospital Specialist

We should do some research on the causes of accidents.

Company Labour Officer

It's been a place of hazard for ages - don't really know why?

Worker

Accidents will happen

A Group of Workers

Trainee

The work's all right. I think older people are just careless.

Accidents per 100 employees 1989/90		
Firm	Men	Women
Lemans	29	37
Production	3	27
Despatch	21	1
Research	2	2
Offices	3	7
Warrens	13	11
GMB Engineering	15	7
Repro Ltd	16	6

Female Worker

"I feel so tired - it's always so warm. You just fall asleep sometimes."

Surely Health and Safety should have been considered long ago!

Office Worker

Isn't the situation better than it used to be?

Van Drivers

We must hold courses on safety.

Union Official

Now complete the following stages.

Stage 1: Identify the Task

....

Stage 2: Layout

To: ....

From: ....

Date: ....

Subject: ....

Appropriate headings for this task are: ....

Stage 3: Identify Relevant Information

....

....

....

....

....

....

....

....

....

....

....

....

Stage 4: Group/Order Relevant Information

....

....

....

....

....

....

....

....

....

....

....

Stage 5: Write the Report

Stage 6: Check your Work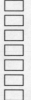

Checklist: Report

1	Have you completed the task?	☐
2	Is the layout you have chosen appropriate for the task?	☐
3	Is the information relevant?	☐
4	Is the information in the right order?	☐
5	Is the language appropriate?	☐
6	Have you given some recommendations?	☐
7	Have you checked spelling, grammar and punctuation?	☐

SECTION 3: Short Answers

Introduction

The type of question requiring short answers always appears in Question 3.

Stage 1: Identify the Task

There is often a lot of text/information in this question. Before you start to read this, look at the instructions carefully to see exactly what you have to do and what kind of answers are required. You are normally asked to "Answer the questions which follow the text".

Stage 2: How to Complete the Task

When you have read through the task, do not panic when you see a lot of text. It is as important to be able to pick out specific information as to ignore irrelevant information from the authentic piece of text given. You are also asked to answer specific questions only, so do not panic if you find a lot of new words. Try and guess what they mean. If you can't, ignore them.

The best approach once you have read the instructions is:

1   Read **all** the questions first.
2   Read **all** the text before answering any questions.
3   Read the questions one at a time and look for specific answers.

Remember:

-   the information in the text is not always in the same order as in the questions
-   make sure you give the information you are asked for
-   if you can't answer a question, go on to the next and come back to it later

It is important that the answers are as brief as possible, eg incomplete sentences, figures, single words, etc.

Stage 3: How to Answer

Make sure all answers are clearly numbered and easy to read.

Stage 4: Check your Work

Checklist: Short Answers

The following is a list of points to check when you give short answers.

1   Have you completed the task?
2   Have you clearly numbered your answers?
3   Have you answered in short sentences?
4   Have you answered all the questions?
5   Have you checked spelling, grammar and punctuation?

Practice 1

As an employee of the European Community working in EC offices in Brussels, you have been asked to research Electronic Banking Systems. Attempting to be helpful, a colleague passes you the article below and poses some questions which he feels may give greater understanding of factors involved.

Answer the questions which follow the text.

Stage 1: Identify the Task

Answer the questions which follow the text.

Stage 2: Before you Start

Have you read through **all** the questions?
Have you read through **all** the information?

Electronic Banking - Payment Systems

Considerable progress has been made throughout the EC in the use of electronic payment cards in Automated Telling Machines (ATMs); they are now used in all 12 Member States. At present, however, not every country has machines that accept all the most widely used cards carried by both business and leisure travellers. In fact, only France and Spain have networks of machines which will accept both Eurocards, Eurocheque cards and Visa cards.

Nexus

One company which is at the forefront of the provision of electronic payment equipment is Nexus Payment Systems International. It offers a full range of payment system services to customers who include leading UK and international banks, building societies and major card issuers.

These services include the management and 24 hour support of ATMs and self service banking devices for proprietary and shared networks operational in the UK and other European countries. International ATM connections, Electronic Fund Transfer at Point Of Sale (EFTPOS) and debit card schemes, automated telephone banking, disaster recovery and payment systems consultancy are other mainstream services offered by Nexus to its domestic and international customers.

Eurocheque

An important facility for travellers in the EC is the provision of a new service to enable Nexus UK customers to access all Eurocheque branded ATMs throughout Europe. The service will allow the immediate authorisation of transactions as and when they occur. Rob Farbrother, Managing Director of Nexus explains:

"From Nexus' earliest days, the objective has been to build international cash card routes whereby individual financial institutions give their customers a comprehensive range of cost effective and easy to use European card-based withdrawal and point of sale services."

Continued

"An agreement with Eurocheque provides our customers with access to ATMs in a significant number of European countries, notably 1200 in France and 3240 in Germany. With the increased ease of connection provided by Nexus, combined with the additional cross-border travel of customers, this new development is very important in opening up European payment for millions of British card holders."

National Systems

Apart from the Eurocheque network, Nexus has secured technical gateways into the national electronic payment systems in Spain, Portugal, Italy and Belgium. This will make over 9000 ATMs available for the 11 million UK business travellers and tourists who visit these countries each year. Says Rob Farbrother, "These developments are clearly an important step to making the UK more prepared for the single market. For travellers to receive direct access to their money by use of the very same ATM card issued by a UK bank or building society is a highly valued service."

IBOS

Not all money transactions can be carried out using a plastic card; other cross-border payments such as standing orders, direct debits and other fund transfers can also be made much simpler by using electronic banking systems.

One benefit of the alliance between the Royal Bank of Scotland (RBS) and Banco Santander is a new system called IBOS (Inter Bank Online System). This will allow payments to be made cross-border as easily as between two branches of a bank in the UK - indeed RBS claims that it will be quicker, cheaper and 100 per cent reliable.

The IBOS system, which the banks can license to others, has proprietary software provided by Digital. It works in conjunction with an automated interface unit which enables computers of financial institutions to be connected into the IBOS network as generators and recipients of business.

Source: Single Market News, Spring 1991

(Series 1, 1993, Q3)

Questions

1   What problems currently exist in the use of electronic banking systems in the EC?

2   What does Nexus offer?

3   What do the following stand for?   EFTPOS - IBOS - ATM

4   What does a new service enable Nexus' UK customers to do?

5   What will the new service allow?

6   Where have Nexus secured other gateways into electronic payment systems?

7   What other cross-border payments can be made more easily with electronic systems?

8   To what alliance does IBOS relate?

9   Who provides the software for IBOS?

Stage 3: Write the Answers

1   Only France and Spain have networks of machines which accept the most widely used cards.

2   Nexus offers a full payment system.

3   EFTPOS   -   Electronic Fund Transfer at Point Of Sale

       IBOS   -   Inter Bank Online Service

       ATM   -   Automated Telling Machine

4   Eurocheques can be used at all ATMs in Europe.

5   It will allow immediate authorisation of transfers.

6   In Spain, Portugal, Italy and Belgium.

7   Standing orders, direct debits and other forms of transfers.

8   Between the Royal Bank of Scotland and the Banco Santander.

9   Digital provides the software.

Stage 4: Check your Work ☑

Checklist: Short Answers

1	Have you completed the task?	☑
2	Have you clearly numbered your answers?	☑
3	Have you answered in short sentences?	☑
4	Have you answered all the questions?	☑
5	Have you checked spelling, grammar and punctuation?	☑

Practice 2

At a recent meeting of the oil exporting countries, the paper "Oil and Gas" (produced by the British Foreign and Commonwealth Office) was circulated. Aides are required to prepare notes on the basis of questions posed by ministers. These questions follow the text below. As an aide, answer the questions.

Stage 1:   Identify the Task

Answer the questions which follow the text.

Stage 2:   Before you Start

Have you read through **all** the questions?
Have you read through **all** the information?

Exploration activity in Britain's offshore oil and gas industry remained at a high level in 1989, although oil production fell by nearly 20 per cent and gas production by over 2 per cent. The highest total of exploration and appraisal wells since 1984 were drilled and 29 significant discoveries were made. British suppliers gained 81% of the value of orders for goods and services on the United Kingdom Continental Shelf.

The Government has announced both the twelfth off-shore oil licensing round and the first oil licensing round to encourage exploration in the frontier areas of the North Sea.

The Department of Energy's 1990 review of Britain's oil and gas development also covers economic, industrial, safety and environmental aspects of oil and gas production.

Oil and Gas Production

Britain's total oil production declined from 114.5 million tonnes in 1988 to 91.8 million tonnes in 1989. This latter figure includes 3.7 million tonnes of heavier natural gases, 0.7 million tonnes of condensate and 0.7 million tonnes of onshore crude oil (of which 0.5 million tonnes are produced from the Wytch Farm field and the remainder from minor fields in the East Midlands, Hampshire and Dorset). Eight new offshore oilfields and one onshore oil field (Scampton North in the East Midlands) came onstream in 1989, bringing the total number in production to 44 offshore and 11 onshore fields.

In 1989 gas produced from the United Kingdom Continental Shelf (UKCS) amounted to 44,701 million cubic metres, compared with 45,726 million cubic metres in 1988. Supplies of UKCS gas to British Gas accounted for 79.8 per cent of total supplies (UKCS production plus imports). Four new offshore gas fields came onstream in 1989, bringing the number in production (including one onshore field) to 29.

Exploration and Development

During 1989, 94 exploration and 89 appraisal wells were started. The mature provinces of the North Sea accounted for about 87 per cent of this, drilling activity.

Continued

In 1989, 29 offshore discoveries were announced: 13 of gas, nine of oil, four of oil and gas, two of gas condensate and one of condensate. Onshore, 16 exploration and one appraisal wells were started, and five discoveries made: one in West Sussex, one in the East Midlands, one in North Yorkshire, one in Humberside and one in Strathclyde. The figures for offshore discoveries are the highest since drilling began in the UKCS.

Twelve offshore oil fields, seven offshore gas fields and two onshore oil fields were under development on the UKCS at the end of 1989, and 154 development wells were drilled during the year, 13 less than in 1988, but still more than in any other year.

Reserves

The estimate of proven, plus probable initially recoverable, oil reserves in present discoveries shows a slight increase from 2,380 million tonnes in 1988 to 2,480 million tonnes in 1989. Possible reserves are estimated to remain at 610 million tonnes. The maximum possible total shows a slight increase, from 2,990 million tonnes in 1988 to 3,090 million tonnes in 1989. After taking account of cumulative oil production to the end of 1989 - 1,282 million tonnes - remaining recoverable oil reserves in present discoveries are estimated to be in the range of 510 to 1,810 million tonnes.

Proven, plus probable, plus possible initially recoverable, gas reserves in present discoveries now stand at 2.48 million million cubic metres. Proven, plus probable reserves, have increased from 1.86 million million cubic metres in 1988 to 1.89 million million cubic metres in 1989. After deducting cumulative gas production the end of 1989 of 706,000 million cubic metres, remaining recoverable gas reserves in present discoveries are estimated to be between 560,000 million and 1.77 million million cubic metres.

Potential additional reserves (reserves found by exploration drilling about which insufficient is known to classify them as possible discovered reserves) are put at between 85 million and 210 million tonnes for oil and between 120,000 million and 260,000 million cubic metres for gas.

(Series 4, 1992, Q3)

Questions

1 Which Government Department made this 1990 review?

2 How big were the falls in Britain's offshore oil and gas production in 1989?

3 How did the Government encourage exploration in the frontier areas of the North Sea?

4 What did Britain's total oil production figures of 1989 include?

5 From where did the onshore crude oil in the 1989 figures come?

6 How many oil fields - offshore and onshore - were in production in 1989?

7 What did the offshore discoveries consist of in 1989?

8 How many oil fields and gas fields were under development in 1989?

9 How many development wells were drilled in 1989?

10 What were possible oil reserves estimated to be in 1989?

Stage 3: Write the Answers

1   The British Foreign and Commonwealth Office.

2   Offshore oil fell by nearly 20% and gas by over 2% in 1989.

3   They announced the twelfth offshore oil licensing round and the first oil licensing round to encourage exploration.

4   It includes: 3.7 million tonnes of heavier natural gas
                     0.7 million tonnes of condensate
                     0.7 million tonnes of onshore crude oil.

5   The Wytch Farm field produced 0.5 million tonnes ad the remainder came from minor fields in the East Midlands and Hampshire and Dorset.

6   44 offshore and 11 onshore fields were in production in 1989.

7   Thirteen gas, nine oil, four of oil and gas, two of gas condensate and one of condensate.

8   Twelve offshore oil fields, seven offshore gas fields and two onshore oil fields were under development in 1989.

9   154 development wells were drilled in 1989.

10   Possible reserves are estimated at 610 million tonnes.

Now complete the following stage.

Stage 4: Check your Work ☑

Checklist: Short Answers

1   Have you completed the task?   ☐
2   Have you clearly numbered your answers?   ☐
3   Have you answered in short sentences?   ☐
4   Have you answered all the questions?   ☐
5   Have you checked spelling, grammar and punctuation?   ☐

SECTION 3

Practice 3

Jim Ponsford, Training Officer and Equal Opportunities official at the Northern Merit Bank of Bristol, circulates the text below among colleagues at a staff meeting the bank holds every fortnight. The text will be used as part of a training programme in which you will be involved. Jim Ponsford asks you to make sure that you understand the text by answering the questions which follow.

Stage 1: Identify the Task

Answer the questions which follow the text.

Stage 2: Before you Start

Have you read through **all** the questions?
Have you read through **all** the information?

Third National Bank Takes an Initiative (The Bank Advisor, November 1991)

Third National Bank first established its credentials in promoting equal opportunities when it provided nurseries and creches in three of its branches in 1989. Now, in a series of new and rational developments, it has opened up more areas of opportunity for staff.

One of these developments has been called "Your Progress". It really is a series of self-help, self-development programmes available through branch Training Officers and Staff Libraries. "Your Progress" comes in a set of three packs. Each pack contains booklets and appropriate exercises, together with one or two audio cassettes. The third pack in the series also contains a video cassette (which can be used in branch video machines). The first two packs guide staff into the bank's way of doing things and cover a number of processes and skills which staff are most likely to use at their place of work. The 3rd pack begins to prepare students for banking examinations. It is thought that if students progress to the third pack, then they are committed to a future at the bank.

Incidentally in the packs is the message - continually reinforced - of the bank's positive attitude to equal opportunities. Counselling procedures open to staff are mentioned in the literature and on the tapes.

The Training Officer at the bank's head quarters feels that the packs will help staff and the organisation. "They lay down ground rules for people's futures in the bank and help to allay many of the fears that staff have before they become too big for staff to handle - and naturally we also feel they should take away or at least reduce some of the problem areas that Training Officers and other management staff sometimes encounter in staff", says John Merchant at head quarters.

Other developments from the bank are separate guidelines/booklets for women returning to the bank after a period away. The booklets give information on what is called "Readjustment to Working. So far, the response to these booklets has been very positive. They have caused so much interest, that members of the public have also asked if they could be made available to them.

Continued

"We were among the first banks to make special arrangements for career breaks for women and we then widened that provision to include male staff. I think the bank's management is forward looking enough to realise that life is continually changing and new stresses and strains replace the old ones. So we know that for many committed staff there are still often very great problems outside the bank - birth, bereavement, marriage, house purchase, child illness, child education, and so on. We want the workforce to regard us as acceptable employees but also to see themselves really as part of the bank and indeed part of the employing system.

Without the mass of our employees, there would be no management structure and unless our employees are happy, we have no customers - and the more the bank is interested in its staff, the better the provision all round.

We know the public appreciates our interest in our staff. I think the tremendous range of services we offer the public (to whom we were also among the first to introduce a range of newer customer benefits - interest-bearing accounts, some direct debit provisions free, no commission travellers' cheques for branch customers in the black, and so on) bears this out", John Merchant said.

(Series 3, 1992, Q3)

Questions

1. How did Third National promote equal opportunities at first?
2. Through which bodies is the programme available?
3. What do the first two packs cover?
4. In which pack are banking examinations introduced?
5. How do the packs assist the Training Officers and management staff?
6. How does the Training Officer feel the packs will help staff in banks?
7. What problems exist for staff outside banks?
8. What was the bank among the first to arrange?
9. According to John Merchant, what would there not be without employees?
10. What services was the bank among the first of its kind to introduce?

Now complete the following stages.

Stage 3: Write the Answers

Stage 4:   Check your Work   ☑

Checklist: Short Answers

1	Have you completed the task?	☐
2	Have you clearly numbered your answers?	☐
3	Have you answered in short sentences?	☐
4	Have you answered all the questions?	☐
5	Have you checked spelling, grammar and punctuation?	☐

Practice 4

Trainees in a London Borough's Environmental Health Department are asked by a superior, to make notes on the following article to assist the Chief Officer to make a speech to London Boroughs at a conference on recycling.

As a trainee, help the Chief Officer by answering the questions which follow at the end of the text.

Stage 1: Identify the Task

Answer the questions which follow the text.

Now complete the following stages.

Stage 2: Before you Start

Have you .... ?

Have you .... ?

"New York! New York!" Published by Warmer (World Action for Recycling Materials and Energy from Rubbish) Summer 1990

Recycle, recycle, recycle; indeed recycle. But how to do it in a metropolis the size of New York? This is the challenge faced by municipalities, large and small, across the United States. Each town and county, each city and village is feeling the crunch of dwindling landfill space and further restrictions on the safe incineration of solid waste.

In the United States, recycling, a concept that is as old as it is necessary, has gained increasing momentum. In the last several years, cities like Philadelphia and Los Angeles, as well as New York, have begun kerbside recycling programmes, driven by expensive transport costs of exporting solid waste to distant landfills or in anticipation of legislation. New York City's challenge is all the more difficult because it is truly not one city, but a mix of many small towns and neighbourhoods with one and two family homes, tenement buildings, multiple dwellings, twenty, thirty and even more than forty storey residential buildings and areas where all types of buildings are mixed together. Couple this with the most diverse demographics of perhaps any city in the world in terms of culture, language and economics and the problem becomes even more focused.

The mechanism to meet the recycling challenge in New York City is its Department of Sanitation. The department collects 10,000 - 24,000 tons of residential refuse with some 6,000 truck shifts weekly. A truck shift consists of an eight hour working period for a crew and its equipment.

What to Recycle?

Because of its abundance and ripe existing markets, newspaper was identified as the first and most recyclable item in New York's waste stream. Additionally metal and glass food containers, corrugated cardboard, magazines and plastics were selected as eminently recyclable items.

Continued

Where to Recycle?

New York City is divided into 59 community sanitation districts. The population served in each district varies from less than 100,000 to more than 200,000 persons. When a district is selected for recycling, the department notifies its residents that recycling is coming to their neighbourhood. Letters are mailed to explain the need to recycle, to bundle and tie newspapers, to rinse out metal cans and glass bottles and the days of the recycling collection service. Posters are placed in shop windows and lobbies. Department personnel speak to community and civic groups, churches, schools and other local organisations. This public education is essential for successful participation in a recycling programme. Prior to a district being placed on recycling, the department's Operations Assistance Unit designs recycling collection routes. Consideration is given to the amount of waste generated in the district, a projection of existing recyclables in the waste stream, the number of refuse collection stops in the area and an estimate of public participation.

The recycling Operations Unit is the unit responsible for managing personnel and equipment engaged in the daily collection and transport of recyclables. The office assigns and monitors the number of recycling trucks each district uses, as well as type and size. Districts with a large volume of recyclables use the standard rear loading collection trucks. Districts with lesser volume use a bin type recycling truck which is especially good for metal and glass collection.

(Series 2, 1992, Q3)

Questions

1   What restrictions are faced by municipalities in carrying out recycling?

2   Give examples of cities involved in recycling processes in the USA.

3   What factors have acted as incentives to those carrying out recycling programmes?

4   Why does New York have such a problem with the challenge of recycling?

5   Which sector of government carries out recycling in New York?

6   Identify those commodities worth recycling.

7   Which areas assist the recycling process in New York?

8   What is used by districts which have less recyclable waste than other areas?

9   What is described as "essential" for a successful recycling programme?

10   As well as collection routes, what other factors are considered before a district is placed on recycling?

Stage 3:   Write the Answers

Stage 4:   Check your Work

Checklist: Short Answers

1   Have you completed the task?
2   Have you clearly numbered your answers?
3   Have you answered in short sentences?
4   Have you answered all the questions?
5   Have you checked spelling, grammar and punctuation?

Practice 5

At a recent conference, students studying Anglo-French trade relations were given the text below. Following the reading of the text, they were set certain questions on it. Answer the questions which follow the text.

Now complete the following stages.

Stage 1: Identify the Task

....

Stage 2: Before you Start

Have you .... ?

Have you .... ?

Selling to France (Single Market News)

France is the UK's third largest customer in the world, accounting for around 10% of our total overseas trade. Recently, there has been a significant shift in the nature of British trade with France, away from petroleum and related products and towards manufactured goods, with market share in the service sector also growing.

Invisibles and Investment Opportunities

There are now more than 2,000 British companies with established subsidiaries or other forms of investment in France. With the advancement of the Channel Tunnel and the completion of the single market in view, the scope for further industrial and commercial collaboration is sure to increase.

The presence in France of British banking interest, insurance companies, property developers and legal practitioners continues to grow. In the invisible sector as well as in industry and commerce the trend is increasingly towards a form of partnership arrangement with French companies.

The Department of Trade and Industry's French desk has a number of publications available to guide business on trading with France:

France	-	A Country Profile
France	-	Hints to Exporters
France	-	Agency Legislation
France	-	Forming a Company

Further useful information available from DTI includes handouts on French regulatory matters, from rates of TVA (Value Added Tax) to permitted additives in various foodstuffs.

Consumer Products

The French market for consumer goods is similar to that in the UK. Although methods of distribution and local tastes vary, with sound marketing practices almost anything can be sold. Demand for gardening and Do It Yourself equipment is expanding rapidly; good quality British food and drink products are increasingly popular; and classical British clothing and more recently contemporary British fashion design are much appreciated in the French market place. Another area where British goods are becoming popular is the giftware, chinaware, jewellery and gift stationery sector.

Continued

UK sports manufacturers should be aware that golf is now the fastest growing sport in France. The number of players is expected to double by 1992. However, competition is strong from the USA and Japan and British manufacturers are advised to research that market carefully and develop distribution channels as soon as possible.

Relevant publications from the Department of Trade and Industry's French desk are:

Marketing Consumer Goods in France

Mail Order Houses in France

Market Reports and Summaries on: Giftware
Do It Yourself
Tableware
Business and Promotional Gifts
Furniture
Gardening Equipment
Domestic Electrical Appliances
Sportswear

Capital Goods

The most successful British suppliers to the French market are those who produce top quality goods. There is a steady if not increasing demand for machine tools, medical equipment, security equipment, pollution control equipment, and an aftermarket for car components and accessories. Other areas of interest include aerospace components, printing and packaging equipment, electronic testing and measuring equipment and information technology. DTI's French desk has market reports on: machine goods
health care
construction
scientific instruments
computers
water industry/pollution control

(Series 1, 1992, Q3)

Questions

1   What changes have occurred in the kinds of British trade with France?

2   What will enhance the scope for further collaboration?

3   What trend is recognisable in the invisible sector?

4   What publications are available to assist business in trading with France?

5   Give examples of useful supplementary information that is available to businesses.

6   From where would the British find competition in promoting golf products in France?

7   What are the British advised to do to combat competition in golf products?

8   Although the French market for consumer goods is similar to the British market, what variations might there be in France?

9   Who are the most successful British suppliers to France?

10   In the Capital goods sector, for what goods is there a steady demand?

SECTION 3

Stage 3: Write the Answers

Stage 4: Check your Work ☑

Checklist: Short Answers

1	Have you completed the task?	☐
2	Have you clearly numbered your answers?	☐
3	Have you answered in short sentences?	☐
4	Have you answered all the questions?	☐
5	Have you checked spelling, grammar and punctuation?	☐

Practice 6

Pilar Milverton has money to spare and wants to get the maximum benefits in savings. Her husband obtains the following details from the Money Show in London. Pilar, who is very careful but not sure of her English, has a number of questions which she wishes to ask her husband about the article. These follow the article below.

Now complete the following stages.

Stage 1: Identify the Task

....

Stage 2: Before you Start

Have you .... ?

Have you .... ?

Profitable Niche (Financial Times, 23 September 1989)

Jay Gross, chairman of an American savings bank, Bell Savings Bank of Philadelphia, is hoping to double his British and West German trading this year in a niche market for small businesses that he has made his bank's overseas speciality.

Bell Savings is one of the rare institutions that are prepared to handle, without prohibitive transaction fees, accounts for small businesses whose trade involves a number of small cheques in US dollars. By running everything from the bank's head office in Philadelphia, and by cutting costs to the bone, Gross is turning what began as a novelty into a serious international market for his bank.

Gross now has 4,000 small businesses and individual depositors based in Britain, and a slightly higher number in Germany. He concluded negotiations with the Swiss and Dutch authorities two weeks ago and expects to start offering the service in those countries shortly. He expects his British and German business to double this year and hopes to be providing low cost dollar banking for small value transactions throughout Europe by 1992.

Gross has found his market by turning conventional US commercial banking practice on its head. The US banks do not like accounts with a great many small cheques passing through them, unless arrangements are made and fees are established to cover the paper handling. US accounts are often geared to a limit of a certain number of transactions per month, depending upon the size of the funds deposited.

In contrast, Bell Savings Bank has built its domestic business upon small transactions in the 50 years since it was founded by the Gross family. It has almost $1 billion total assets, of which more than $700 million is represented by small deposits averaging about $6,000. "We have traditionally geared ourselves to handle accounts of that size involving numerous small transactions", says Gross.

Continued

The bank has staff of 400 in 20 offices in Philadelphia. Small business depositors in Europe keep in touch by using a toll-free telephone number to the Philadelphia head quarters. Customers usually pay in their dollar cheques by post. They are not debited for any currency conversion charges. The free line has proved a piece of inspired public relations for Bell Savings. When European customers visit the US, they are apt to call in to the Philadelphia office to greet the women clerks who handle their accounts. Sometimes they take flowers. "I think some of them call in just to see if we are for real", Gross laughs.

The bank accepts a minimum opening deposit of £500 and can pay withdrawals either by wire or by sterling cheque sent through the post. Customers can also have access to their money in Britain and other countries outside the US by using a cash card geared to the Link system. Interest rates paid on deposits vary slightly according to the type of account chosen.

As for security, each account is insured for up to $100,000 with the Federal Deposit Insurance Corporation, a US Government agency.

If you are travelling a great deal, and paying hotel and similar bills in US dollars, it might be worth considering taking out an American Express international dollar card linked to a Bell Savings account. You will avoid suffering currency conversion at often onerous rates.

The card can be used for purchases in any currency but must be settled in dollars. It can be paid direct from the Bell bank account.

(Series 4, 1991, Q3)

Now answer Pilar Milverton's questions.

Questions

1   What performance is the chairman hoping to achieve?
2   With whom is Bell Savings willing to do business?
3   What kind of depositors does Bell have in Britain, Spain and Europe generally?
4   With which countries has Bell negotiated so far?
5   What does Gross hope to offer by the early 1990s?
6   How did Gross discover this market?
7   What do most of his assets represent?
8   How do customers maintain contact with the bank?
9   How has the telephone system proved to be inspired?
10   How can withdrawals be made?

Stage 3: Write the Answers

Stage 4: Check your Work ☑

Checklist: Short Answers

1   Have you completed the task? ☐
2   Have you clearly numbered your answers? ☐
3   Have you answered in short sentences? ☐
4   Have you answered all the questions? ☐
5   Have you checked spelling, grammar and punctuation? ☐

Practice 7

You work for a firm of travel agents. One day your manager notices a leaflet on the "Heathrow Express" and feels that the sooner staff in the firm know about it, the better they will be able to answer questions from the public. In order to ensure that staff digest the information in the leaflet he says, at a staff meeting "Read this leaflet thoroughly. Then answer my questions which follow. I want brief, readable answers - no padding. There is a prize for the best answers."

Comply with your manager's request.

Now complete the following stages.

Stage 1:   Identify the Task

....

Stage 2:   Before you Start

Have you .... ?

Have you .... ?

The Heathrow Express - Railway to the Air

High quality service for Britain's premier airport.
Reinforces BAA's commitment to passenger service.
Environmentally sound with minimal disturbance to Green Belt land.
Will ease congestion on the roads and overcrowding on the underground.
Wheelchairs and trolleys can be wheeled to platform level.
Comfortable, spacious rolling stock designed for the air traveller.
Trains every 15 minutes from 0500 to 2330 hours.
Fast, direct service to all four airport terminals - 16 minutes from Paddington to Terminals 1,2 and 3, and 20 minutes to Terminal 4.

In line with its futuristic rail shuttle between the main terminal and the satellite at Gatwick Airport, BAA - The British Airports Authority - has put forward proposals to build a high speed rail link between Heathrow Airport and Paddington Station (London's major rail terminal for West Country rail services). These proposals are now with Parliament, where the benefits that the new rail link will provide, and the care taken in its planning, are being emphasised.

The Heathrow Express rail link project has been designed to enhance the level of customer service at Heathrow, the world's premier international airport. Every quarter of an hour throughout the day it will speed travellers between London's West End and Heathrow Airport - taking just 16 minutes. Initial estimates indicate that the service will carry six million passengers each year.

Continued

The total costs of the project are estimated at £235 million. This will be funded by BAA (80%) and its partners, British Rail Network South East (20%). The partnership will reflect a unique combination of private and public sectors of the economy. Revenue from fares charged will be at a premium rate to cover costs and produce a return on investment made.

In developing the project, the twin priorities of customer comfort and concern for the environment have been fully considered. The new trains - owned by BAA - will have interiors especially designed for air travellers and BAA staff will provide a high quality service both on board and at the stations. As the trains will be electronically powered, they will be significantly quieter than diesel stock currently in service on similar routes. For most of its length, the branch line - for that is what it will be - will run under the M4 and in a tunnel. The link will certainly ease congestion on the roads and overcrowding on the underground to Heathrow.

Improvements considered for Paddington include changes to traffic circulation in and around the station area and new arrangements for taxis.

In 1988, the Government approved the scheme in principle - after very close scrutiny of the other routes proposed. The Heathrow Express Bill is currently under consideration by Parliament. If the latest proposals are approved, the first train could be running by late 1993.

(Series 3, 1991, Q3)

Questions

1   How will the express affect the environment?

2   What features will assist the disabled?

3   What is considered significant in the proposals before Parliament?

4   From where will most of the finance for the project be forthcoming?

5   Why is the partnership of BAA and British Rail unusual?

6   How are fares on the project to be set?

7   What priorities have been considered in the project?

8   Where will BAA staff provide effective service?

9   How will the system aid the environment and problems of congestion?

10   How did the government approve of the scheme?

Stage 3: Write the Answers

Stage 4: Check your Work ☑

Checklist: Short Answers

1	Have you completed the task?	☐
2	Have you clearly numbered your answers?	☐
3	Have you answered in short sentences?	☐
4	Have you answered all the questions?	☐
5	Have you checked spelling, grammar and punctuation?	☐

Practice 8

"This is turning the clock back", said James McCafferty, Business degree course leader at Singleton University in Wales. "Here we are trying to promote competence testing - and this is what we see. What I'd like you to do is to see if this article (in full below) really pinpoints the problems. In that connection I've drafted some questions I'd like you to test against the article."

As James McCafferty's assistant, write notes in response to the questions he sets. The questions follow the article.

Now complete the following stages.

Stage 1: Identify the Task

....

Stage 2: Before you Start

Have you .... ?

Have you .... ?

Travel Agents By-Pass Competence Testing

According to various informed sources in the travel trade, only one travel agent in ten is testing adequately for technical skills and competence with new staff. This is according to a recent survey highlighted in the travel press.

High turnover of staff, low wages and a heavy dependency on temps (staff temporarily employed) are also revealed as the "downside" of employment in the travel industry. This confirms many opinions of low professionalism in the travel trade. Publications concerning pay in London give the following figures.

London staff pay (a year):		
	Juniors	£6,000
	Clerks (2 years)	£8,500
	Senior Clerks	£10,800
	Assistant Managers	£13,000
	Managers	£14,730

In many cases, pay for travel agency staff is low compared with workers undertaking similar work in commercial offices. In a number of instances it may be supposed to be much more in line with staff working in the Distribution Trade generally.

While it seems 80% of the agencies interviewed preferred staff with professional qualifications, just 11% tested them for competence, ie for skills used in travel agency work.

"Only a few would try them on Travicom or do proper written test. I would have thought at least half would, but the figures were a real surprise", said Julia Feuell, area manager for T&T Travel Personnel.

Continued

That particular company, for its survey, sent out questionnaires to 500 London travel agencies from which 72% responded to T & T T (which provides temporary or full time travel staff) as follows:

What agencies do:	Car Hire	88%
	Tailor-made Holidays	88%
	Hotel Reservations/	82%
	Package Holidays	

| **What agencies don't do:** | British Rail Bookings | 73% |
| | Incoming Arrangements | 67% |

Turnover in staff in the capital is worrying. At four per year it is high - but this is down on the previous year's figure of 4.8. Most agencies are hoping for a further drop.

"The figure is still very high. It appears whereas staff used to move every couple of years, it is now more like 18 months. It isn't an industry where you stay in a job ten years then move", said Ms Feuell.

Two thirds of retailers use temporary staff, while 34% have staff willing to work overtime. This is sometimes reflected in the image presented to the public - which in some agencies is often a little less than welcoming. Hence the value placed upon professionals.

The age of the average staff member is 25 and each works 37.5 hours each week. Some 75% of agencies also offer some form of bonuses or incentives to staff.

But while the survey revealed that staff are offered two "educationals" a year (ie training sessions or travel), 45% of bosses impose restrictions on when they can be taken.

(Series 2, 1991, Q3)

Questions

1   What accounts for low professionalism in the industry?

2   Whom do most agencies prefer as staff?

3   Do agencies test new staff?

4   Why were the figures revealed by the survey a surprise?

5   On average, how much better off is a manager than a junior in a travel agency in London?

6   What services do T & T provide for agencies?

7   What are the patterns of staff turnover in London agencies?

8   What work will most agencies not do?

9   What do the policies of most agencies appear to be in respect of: (a) temporary staff

(b) incentives to staff?

10   What policies do agencies have in respect of "educationals"?

Stage 3:   Write the Answers

Stage 4:   Check your Work

Checklist: Short Answers

1	Have you completed the task?	☐
2	Have you clearly numbered your answers?	☐
3	Have you answered in short sentences?	☐
4	Have you answered all the questions?	☐
5	Have you checked spelling, grammar and punctuation?	☐

Practice 9

Women meeting for an international seminar at a congress centre in Westminster are handed the article below and asked to complete the questions that follow prior to a discussion later in the day.

Answer the questions they are given which follow the text.

Now complete the following stages.

Stage 1: Identify the Task

....

Stage 2: Before you Start

Have you .... ?

Have you .... ?

Aid Projects Bring Hope for Women in the Third World

In the least developed countries in the world, about 30 per cent of the rural households are headed by women, who are the sole supporters of their families. The 35th session of the UN Commission on the Status of Women, meeting in Vienna on March 4, heard a plea from Dr Idriss Jazairy, President of the Rome based International Fund for Agricultural Development (IFAD), for a "concerted effort to ensure that (these) women are... an integral part of project design", reports Ali Al-Khazraji, OPECNA International Fora Editor.

Dr Jazairy, who was addressing the opening session of the conference with a presentation on the economic advancement of rural women, said that IFAD was initiating efforts worldwide for all of its projects to take account of the needs of women, to ensure their equal access to both financial and technical assistance. "This has become essential since IFAD studies have shown that among the world's poorest, rural women predominate." The improvement of their situation has been one of the principal priorities of the Fund in the developing and least developed countries since its inception in 1977. IFAD had made it part of its strategy to provide these poor households with credit, and to match these loans with technical assistance, training and agricultural skills that will enable these women to lighten their workload and allow them to earn. In future, the Fund will earmark 30 per cent of its resources to reach women within all project activities by 1992.

Our projects are aimed at combating hunger and malnutrition and thus upholding a fundamental right, the right of all people to have enough to eat and to ensure minimum nutritional requirements for their children... in this regard, poor rural women have a key role to play."

Continued

Lack of Support

The majority of the world's poorest he noted, were women. Moreover, in many regions, the backlash of the national adjustment processes was now actually worsening their situation. Burdened by heavy domestic responsibilities, an increasing number of women were *de facto* smallholder heads of households, yet rarely possessed an equitable share of local resources, too rarely got training or the financial and technical support they needed to become more productive and self reliant.

"They have no legal tenure to the land they work, often they are barred from receiving credit, ignored by extension services, and under represented in rural associations and decision making bodies", he said.

He said IFAD's planning was based on three approaches: some projects were aimed solely at women, others had women as primary beneficiaries, and the third tried to ensure that rural women received an appropriate share of project benefits.

In 1984, he said, half of the Fund's projects included specific components for women, while in recent years, the proportion had exceeded 90 per cent. By the end of 1989, IFAD had extended $2.9 billion or 25 per cent to help finance 266 projects worth $11.1 billion in 93 countries, spreading across the developing world.

In 1989 alone, IFAD extended $259 million in 25 loans plus $12.5 million in 31 grants, bringing the grant total to $272.4 million since its inception in 1978.

(Source: OPEC Bulletin, March 1991)

(Series 3, 1993, Q3)

Questions

1   What, according to Dr Jazairy, was IFAD starting to do?

2   Where do rural women predominate?

3   Since when has the improvement in the situation of rural women been a major priority of the fund?

4   What does IFAD aim to do through its projects?

5   What proportion of the fund's projects have included specific provision for women in recent years?

6   On what was IFAD's planning based?

7   What fundamental right did IFAD, according to Dr Jazairy, aim to uphold?

8   At the end of 1989, for how many projects in how many countries had IFAD provided financial assistance?

9   What percentage of its resources will IFAD earmark to reach women within all projects by 1992?

10   What did Dr Jazairy indicate about women's ownership of land and the right to receive credit?

Stage 3: Write the Answers

Stage 4: Check your Work ☑

Checklist: Short Answers

1 Have you completed the task? ☐
2 Have you clearly numbered your answers? ☐
3 Have you answered in short sentences? ☐
4 Have you answered all the questions? ☐
5 Have you checked spelling, grammar and punctuation? ☐

Practice 10

To assist understanding at a conference on government statistical provision, you are handed the article below. To aid comprehension, you are asked to tackle the questions that follow prior to discussing them immediately after a lecture.

Answer the questions which follow the text.

Now complete the following stages.

Stage 1:   Identify the Task

....

Stage 2:   Before you Start

Have you .... ?

Have you .... ?

Developments in Statistical Computing in the Home Office

The Home Office responsibilities cover a wide range of topics including crime and criminals, the Prison Service and Probation Service, fire, immigration and nationality. The provision of statistics in these areas is carried out by a centralised statistical section consisting of about 200 staff in all and including 29 professional statisticians. In each of these areas of work, a variety of statistics is collected and processed. The results are generally disseminated in written form by publishing bulletins and reports, providing ad hoc advice and briefing, and replying to parliamentary questions and other requests for information.

The statistical staff are arranged in three divisions, Statistics Division 1 deals mainly with crime and criminals; Statistics Division 2 covers the prison and probation services and Statistics Division 3 deals with all other aspects including immigration, nationality, drug misuse, electoral matters and fires. In this last division there is also a small group of staff who provide computer support to staff in all three divisions. The statistical staff are spread over four sites - two sites in central London and two on the outskirts of London.

The Computing Needs of Statistical Work

One of the distinguishing characteristics of statistical work in government is the need to distil large amounts of data into summary form and to disseminate the information and provide advice to those who need it with the minimum of delay. The use of computer facilities in this work is vital and reliance on computer techniques is increasing.

The critical areas in which computers are being used include the following:
(a)   The input and checking of raw data.
(b)   Data aggregation and the identification of trends.
(c)   The preparation of advice and briefing.

Timeliness is the critical factor and this is an area where the increased use of computers has made a major impact on the ability of statistical staff to carry out large amounts of work with limited resources.

Continued

SECTION 3

Developments 1960 - 1990

In the 1960's all statistical computing in the Home Office was carried out on mainframe computers using batch input procedures. The time taken to submit and run a job was usually about 24 hours.

In the 1970's, developments in mainframe computers provided the opportunity to provide users in the Home Office with direct access to the computer to carry out their work. One or two teletype terminals were provided at each statistical site and a booking system introduced. The time taken to complete a computer task was reduced dramatically. There was often, however, a delay of up to 24 hours in the provision of printed output.

From 1981, the facilities for direct access to the mainframe computers from the teletype terminals were gradually replaced by networks of visual display units (workstations). Statistical staff could now access the mainframe from their own office and mainframe printing facilities were installed in the statistical offices to provide immediate printed output. With some of the software packages emerging at that time, the workstations could also be used to carry out some local work, eg word processing, spreadsheet and database facilities.

Apart from word processing, most of the computer work was still carried out on the mainframe computer but it became increasingly obvious that the facilities available on the Home Office mainframe and the statistics divisions' local networks were falling short of those becoming available on personal computers (PCs). A number of stand alone PCs were acquired to provide graphic facilities for the production of charts and overhead transparencies. The introduction of laser printers increased both the speed and quality of printing. As the availability and quality of PC software increased, the use of PCs grew. Times for computing work have improved and can now often be measured in seconds. A booking system was introduced to ensure that the availability of access to the PCs was fairly distributed.

In 1989, plans were drawn up to replace the network of workstations with a network of PCs. The plans were implemented in 1990.

Source: CSO Statistical News, Spring 1991
(Rodney M Taylor, Statistician, Home Office)

(Series 2, 1993, Q3)

Questions

1   Who provides statistics at the Home Office?

2   In what forms are the statistics distributed?

3   How was Home Office statistical computing carried out in the 1960s?

4   What were provided at each statistical site in the 1970s?

5   What delays were frequent in the 1970s in computer tasks?

6   What replaced facilities for direct access to mainframe computers from the teletype terminals in 1981?

7   What local work were workstations enabled to do in 1981?

8   What improved the speed and quality of printing?

9   When were plans implemented to replace a workstation network with a PC network?

Stage 3:   Write the Answers

Stage 4:   Check your Work ☑

Checklist: Short Answers

1	Have you completed the task?	☐
2	Have you clearly numbered your answers?	☐
3	Have you answered in short sentences?	☐
4	Have you answered all the questions?	☐
5	Have you checked spelling, grammar and punctuation?	☐

SECTION 4:   Memos

Introduction

Question 4, according to the Chief Examiner, is "A conversion task: you receive information input in one form - for example, a telex, or letter, or message - and you have to use this information to provide two other forms of communication: a memo, a letter, a telex, a facsimile or whatever." This question is worth 25 points for both answers and so each answer should be about half the length of answers for questions 1, 2 and 3. The memo often occurs as one of the two tasks in Question 4. Other tasks are looked at in Section 5.

Stage 1:   Identify the Task

Read the question and work out exactly what you are required to do. The instructions at the bottom of the question normally read "Write an internal memo" or "Draft the memo".

Stage 2:   Layout

A memo should include the following information:

Who is the memo to?

Who is the memo from?

What is the subject of the memo?
(What the memo is about in a few words.)

What is the date?
(The date on which you are writing.)

These should be positioned as opposite.

```
                    MEMO
To:
From:
Subject:
Date:
```

Stage 3:   Identify Relevant Information

A memo is usually fairly short. It should include enough so that correct information is communicated, but should not include anything extra to this.

Stage 4:   Group/Order Relevant Information

Often the information in the question is presented in a suitable order. Sometimes, however, the different information may be mixed up. In this case it is useful to group information according to themes.

Stage 5:   Write the Memo

Language in memos is shorter and more direct than in a letter. Stay to the point, but be polite.

Stage 6:   Check your Work

Checklist: Memo

The following is a list of points to check when you write a memo.

1   Have you completed the task? (Will the person who receives the memo be able to understand the message?)
2   Is it to the correct person? Is it from the correct person? (Are you writing it under your name?)
3   Does the subject line tell you in a few words what the memo is about?
4   Is it the correct date? (The day of writing.)
5   Have you included all relevant information? (Is any information missing which will hinder understanding of the message?)
6   Have you left out all irrelevant information?
7   Have you grouped/ordered information in the best way?
8   Is the language appropriate for a memo? (Not too polite, but not too short.)
9   Have you checked spelling, grammar and punctuation?

SECTION 4

Practice 1

Below is the transcript of a conversation between Senior Personnel Officer, James Henry, and his Labour Officer, Peter Jones. Both are employed by the nylon spinning firm of Henry Morgan Ltd of Pontypridd in South Wales.

JH	I still can't understand how so many people can be so late so often.
PJ	Well I think more of our staff live further away from the plant than they used to - and the women who have children may be delayed or even absent on occasion. We do employ a lot more women than we used to.
JH	Yes and, of course, those cuts in public bus services don't help. Perhaps we should try to get additional bus services for our workers. I can't see how the buses couldn't make a profit. Of course another alternative is to provide our own bus or even charter one.
PJ	It wouldn't matter so much if the railways up the valley could be relied upon - but trains are often cancelled or delayed. Of course there is also the possibility that many of our workers - especially the part-timers, find the work very monotonous. I often wonder if we couldn't improve things in the production area to keep the workers happy.
JH	I think all the points mentioned have credibility. I think a wise move would be to consult the Works' Union Convenor, Jimmy Smythe, to see what he thinks. He may be able to suggest a number of ideas; though I'm not sure if he'll want to support the part-timers very much. Many of them are not interested in the Union.

Task: Draft a memorandum to Jimmy Smythe, asking if he would like to attend a meeting with James Henry and Peter Jones in the former's office next Friday, 12 September. Indicate the main agenda items which will be considered.

(Series 1, 1993, Q4)

Stage 1: Identify the Task

Draft a memorandum.

Stage 2: Layout

To: Jimmy Smythe - Works' Union Convenor
From: (your name)
Subject: Staff Lateness
Date: 5th September

Stage 3: Identify Relevant Information

- problem of timekeeping
- staff now live further away
- women with children often delayed
- employ more women than formerly
- cuts in public bus services
- possible own bus or charter one
- railways unreliable
- part time production workers
- work monotonous
- meeting with Jimmy Smythe, Works' Union Convenor
- next Friday, 12th September, 10am
- with Peter Jones and James Henry, James Henry's Office

Stage 4: Group/Order Relevant Information

1 Would you like to attend a meeting next Friday 12th September.
2 With James Henry and Peter Jones.
3 In James Henry's office at 10am.
4 Problem of timekeeping.
5 Staff now live further away.
6 Women with children often delayed.
7 Employ more women than formerly.
8 Cuts in public bus services.
9 Possible own bus or charter one.
10 Railways unreliable.
11 Part time production workers.
12 Work monotonous.

Stage 5: Write the Memo

MEMO

To: Jimmy Smythe - Works' Union Convenor

From: (your name)

Subject: Staff Lateness

Date: 5th September

Your are invited to attend a meeting next Friday, 12th September, with James Henry and Peter Jones. The meeting will take place in James Henry's office at 10am.

The main point on the agenda is staff lateness and the possible reasons for this:

-   staff live further away than they used to

-   problems for women with children

-   cuts in public bus services

-   should we provide charter bus?

-   unreliability of train service

-   monotony of job, especially amongst part time production workers.

Perhaps have suggestions how we can tackle this problem.

Stage 6: Check your Work ☑

Checklist: Memo

1	Have you completed the task?	☑
2	Is it to the correct person? Is it from the correct person?	☑
3	Does the subject line tell you in a few words what the memo is about?	☑
4	Is it the correct date?	☑
5	Have you included all relevant information?	☑
6	Have you left out all irrelevant information?	☑
7	Have you ordered the information in the best way?	☑
8	Is the language appropriate for a memo?	☑
9	Have you checked spelling, grammar and punctuation?	☑

SECTION 4

Practice 2

As assistant to the Managing Director of Grow Foods plc, a food production firm, of Afton Vale, Hereford, you receive a telephone call one morning from an official at Buckingham Palace. The call confirms that a Prince of the Royal Family will be visiting the firm on a Thursday in two months' time. You are asked to make arrangements for a visit lasting one and a half hours beginning at 11am on the day (the Prince has another earlier engagement in the vicinity) and "Yes, the royal personage would be happy to spend half an hour of his time at the firm at a buffet lunch with directors at 12 noon but would have to be away promptly at 12.30 pm for another engagement in a town twenty-five miles away. Formal acceptance of his visit will follow shortly."

Your superior is delighted and says "Better get ourselves organised and call a meeting of all the senior managers for Friday next, 15th July. We'll have to tell them to make sure that everything is neat and tidy in all departments on the day; that everyone in the offices comes looking well-dressed and that canteen staff, production shop and transport workers are kept informed and advised of the great honour being done our firm by this visit. Could be a good idea to call meetings of those four areas separately - canteen, offices, production shop and transport - to advise on how the possible disruption of the visit could affect them. Can you see to these points please? I'll let the directors know."

Task: **Circulate a memorandum** to all the senior managers advising them of the royal visit and that their attendance is essential. Give them all details of the visit known at the time your memorandum is circulated and indicate what could be expected of all staff.

(Series 3, 1992, Q4)

Stage 1: Identify the Task
Circulate a memo.

Stage 2: Layout
To: All Senior Managers
From: (your name), Assistant to the Managing Director
Subject: Royal Visit
Date: 8th July

Stage 3: Identify Relevant Information
- royal visit
- Thursday in 2 months' time
- 1½ hrs, starting 11 am
- tour of factory
- buffet lunch with directors 12 noon
- meeting Friday next on 15th July
- everything neat and tidy
- everyone well-dressed
- staff informed of what's going on
- great honour
- call separate meeting for four areas - canteen, offices, production shop and transport - to look at possible disruption caused by visit

Stage 4: Group/Order Relevant Information
1. Royal visit.
2. Great honour.
3. Thursday in 2 months' time.
4. 1½ hours starting 11 am.
5. Tour of factory.
6. Buffet lunch with directors 12 noon.
7. Meeting Friday next on 15th July.
8. Everything neat and tidy.
9. Everyone well-dressed.
10. Staff informed of what's going on.
11. Call separate meetings for four areas - canteen, offices, production shop and transport - to look at possible disruption caused by visit.

Stage 5:   Write the Memo

MEMO

To: All Senior Managers

From: (your name), Assistant to the Managing Director

Subject: Royal Visit

Date: 8th July

We have just been informed that a Prince of the Royal Family will visit our firm. This is a great honour for us. The visit will take place on a Thursday in 2 months' time and will last for 1½ hours, starting at 11 am. The Prince will tour the factory and at 12 noon, have a buffet lunch in the canteen with our directors. A meeting has been called for Friday next, the 15th July.

On the day of the visit everything must be neat and tidy and everyone well-dressed. It is important to keep staff informed of what is going on and it would be a good idea to call separate meetings for the four areas - canteen/offices/production shop and transport, to look at possible disruptions caused by the Royal Visit.

Now complete the following stage.

Stage 6:   Check your Work   ☑

Checklist: Memo

1	Have you completed the task?	☐
2	Is it to the correct person? Is it from the correct person?	☐
3	Does the subject line tell you in a few words what the memo is about?	☐
4	Is it the correct date?	☐
5	Have you included all relevant information?	☐
6	Have you left out all irrelevant information?	☐
7	Have you ordered the information in the best way?	☐
8	Is the language appropriate for a memo?	☐
9	Have you checked spelling, grammar and punctuation?	☐

SECTION 4

Practice 3

The following is a conversation between the Advertising Manager, Mr James Attridge, and one of his assistants, Miss Petra Angelis, in the firm of Attridge and Barnaby, advertising agents.

> JA   Morning Petra. Any ideas yet about the project for Pearlsons' soap advertising campaign?
>
> PA   I've had a few - some of them unworkable. But there is an idea I'd like to try.
>
> JA   Well what is it - how much does it cost? I think the logistics are important to work out.
>
> PA   Oh, I agree. So what I'd like to do is to use that well-tried formula of consumer testing. You know - like the ones where you test the use of a commodity and prove by various means that ours is best. It's been tried to test the taste of margarine too.
>
> JA   Yes, I see... but if it's been tried before, isn't it a bit old hat and won't people think we're just jumping on the bandwagon?
>
> PA   To some extent; but I thought we could go beyond that. After the consumer testing, we could actually take the consumers and show them precisely how the soap is made, how it is developed - and so on. This might be a step ahead of those companies who just show the consumers being very pleased with the soap. We could present our adverts in two parts. Perhaps they could be a little longer than usual but when people get used to our presentations on TV and elsewhere, we could show either part of the advertisement - separately- rather like that marvellous dog food advert which sometimes shows a part or whole sequence of the dogs scampering across moorland. In time people would be aware of the whole sequence. If past efforts of a similar nature are anything to go by, sales should soar.
>
> JA   Right - let's plan it in detail.

Task: Draft a memorandum inviting members of the Marketing and Finance Departments to a preliminary meeting.

(Series 4, 1991, Q4)

Stage 1: Identify the Task
Draft a memo.

Stage 2: Layout

To: Marketing and Finance
From: (your name)
Subject: Advertising campaign for Pearlson's soap
Date: (today's date)

Stage 3: Identify Relevant Information

- invite Marketing and Finance Departments to preliminary meeting
- suggest date/time/place
- reason for meeting
- ideas for campaign
- notify if cannot attend

Stage 4: Group/Order Relevant Information

1   Meeting to be held.
2   Monday 12th July, 11am.
3   Mr Attridge's office.
4   Ideas for soap advertising campaign.
5   Notify if you cannot attend.

Now complete the following stages.

Stage 5:   Write the Memo

Stage 6:   Check your Work ☑

Checklist: Memo

1   Have you completed the task?   ☐
2   Is it to the correct person? Is it from the correct person?   ☐
3   Does the subject line tell you in a few words what the memo is about?   ☐
4   Is it the correct date?   ☐
5   Have you included all relevant information?   ☐
6   Have you left out all irrelevant information?   ☐
7   Have you ordered the information in the best way?   ☐
8   Is the language appropriate for a memo?   ☐
9   Have you checked spelling, grammar and punctuation?   ☐

Practice 4

You are the Personal Assistant of Alexander Browtin, Managing Director of Univax International's UK subsidiary. Just before he jets off to a meeting with overseas interests, the MD says:

"I've just heard that finance for research and development next year is to be cut by at least a third. Call a meeting of HoDs for Tuesday next to discuss resource implications. It is imperative all attend the meeting and likely that several projects face the axe. Ask all attending to suggest possible areas. It will be useful to call in Winsey who's on leave (get his address from staffing). Tell him we'll get him back there quickly afterwards. It might be useful to call in Sam, the Works' Convenor - just to put him in the picture. I almost forgot - the Head of Personnel's on holiday in Germany. Phone him at his hotel - give him the chance to come over if he thinks it advisable.

You'd better make the meeting for 12 noon on the day with sandwiches, coffee etc. See if anybody needs accommodation for the night before - and try to ensure everyone's prepared.

Task: Draft the memo calling the meeting.

(Series 3, 1991, Q4)

Stage 1: Identify the Task

Draft the memo.

Stage 2: Layout

To: All Heads of Departments
From: (your name), Personal Assistant to MD
Subject: Proposed Cuts in Research and Development
Date: (today's date)

Stage 3: Identify Relevant Information

- finance for Research and Development to be cut by at least a third

- meeting next Tuesday in boardroom to discuss resource implications

- imperative all attend

- likely that several projects will be axed

- need suggestions for possible areas

- 12 noon

- sandwiches/coffee provided

- accommodation needs

Now complete the following stages.

Stage 4: Group/Order Relevant Information

....
....
....
....
....
....
....
....
....
....
....

Stage 5: Write the Memo

Stage 6: Check your Work ☑

Checklist: Memo

1	Have you completed the task?	☐
2	Is it to the correct person? Is it from the correct person?	☐
3	Does the subject line tell you in a few words what the memo is about?	☐
4	Is it the correct date?	☐
5	Have you included all relevant information?	☐
6	Have you left out all irrelevant information?	☐
7	Have you ordered the information in the best way?	☐
8	Is the language appropriate for a memo?	☐
9	Have you checked spelling, grammar and punctuation?	☐

Practice 5

John Walker, the Managing Director of Elsom Export plc of Birmingham, is angry and disconsolate. He declares with some vehemence:

"This company is losing a lot of money when our sales reps go into Europe. I've just had a report from our insurers; they intend to raise our insurance premiums for overseas travel because our reps in Europe are making too much use of private medical facilities for minor ailments - and these are very costly. They should be using state medical services for minor matters in EEC countries. All they need is Form E111. They must abide by the same system we offer them at home; private medical care for major health problems and the National Health Service for coughs and colds. It might be a good idea too for them to check what they need in the way of injections and medicines in other countries when they're about to go away.

Another thing is that too many of our reps are changing English money abroad anywhere they happen to be. This is expensive and wasteful. We have facilities here for arranging foreign currency. Why aren't they using travellers' cheques (we provide them) and credit cards? They're safer than cash. Tell them too, that if they don't stop these wasteful ways, heads will roll. Job losses will soon cure them!"

As your Managing Director's PA, you listen to this tirade and then tackle the following task:

Draft a memorandum to be circulated to all sales representatives indicating the above practices must cease.

(Series 2, 1991, Q4)

Stage 1: Identify the Task	Stage 2: Layout
Draft the memo.	To: All Sales Representatives
	From: (your name), Personal Assistant to MD
	Subject: Reps in Europe - medical and currency facilities
	Date: (today's date)

Now complete the following stages.

Stage 3: Identify Relevant Information	Stage 4: Group/Order Relevant Information
....	....
....	....
....	....
....	....
....	....
....	....
....	....
....	....
....	....
....	....

Stage 5: Write the Memo

Stage 6: Check your Work ☑

Checklist: Memo

1	Have you completed the task?	☐
2	Is it to the correct person? Is it from the correct person?	☐
3	Does the subject line tell you in a few words what the memo is about?	☐
4	Is it the correct date?	☐
5	Have you included all relevant information?	☐
6	Have you left out all irrelevant information?	☐
7	Have you ordered the information in the best way?	☐
8	Is the language appropriate for a memo?	☐
9	Have you checked spelling, grammar and punctuation?	☐

Practice 6

You are the Safety Officer of SH Gruber, stove manufacturers of the Wirral Trading Estate, Birkenhead, Cheshire, BN13 4SJ. A serious accident is reported to you - a machinist has lost his left hand in an accident in the production shop. You visit the production shop and say to yourself:

> The machine is very poorly maintained, too much grease and not enough in the right places. Protecting cover for the arms and face appears to have been removed. Oil around the machine and on the floor.
>
> It's a good job there are no H & S Inspectors around.

You talk to the foreman: (S = self / F = foreman)

S	"What was Hopkins, the machinist wearing?"
F	"Gloves."
S	"That's all right. Hasn't he got long hair?"
F	"Yes, it was tied up in an elastic band."
S	"(Thinks): I don't believe it. Now I recall he's also been for eye tests recently."
S	"Had he been drinking?"
F	"Probably had a couple at lunch time!"
S	"Incredible! He knows these machines must be operated with extreme caution!"

Afterwards, your suggestions include: arranging a meeting for all production staff; ensuring the Health & Safety Acts are posted everywhere; that company requirements for safety are known to all; and making sure that nobody is stupid enough to flout regulations whilst wearing inappropriate dress or hairstyles.

Task: Draft a memorandum reporting the incident and your reactions to the Managing Director.

(Series 1, 1991, Q4)

Stage 1: Identify the Task

Draft the memo.

Now complete the following stages.

Stage 2: Layout

To: ....

From: ....

Subject: ....

Date: ....

Stage 3:   Identify Relevant Information

....
....
....
....
....
....
....
....
....
....
....
....
....
....
....

Stage 4:   Group/Order Relevant Information

....
....
....
....
....
....
....
....
....
....
....
....
....
....

Stage 5: Write the Memo

Stage 6: Check your Work ☑

Checklist: Memo

1 Have you completed the task?
2 Is it to the correct person? Is it from the correct person?
3 Does the subject line tell you in a few words what the memo is about?
4 Is it the correct date?
5 Have you included all relevant information?
6 Have you left out all irrelevant information?
7 Have you ordered the information in the best way?
8 Is the language appropriate for a memo?
9 Have you checked spelling, grammar and punctuation?

Practice 7

The following telephone conversation takes place between James Moxon of RCB Satellites Ltd and Professor Peter Clinton of the Telecoms Research Institute, 25 Bedford Square, London, WC1J 3BX.

Moxon	Good morning, Professor Clinton, James Moxon here - from RCB. Do you remember? We met at the Telecoms Conference last year.
Professor	Yes I do, of course. What can I do for you, Mr Moxon?
Moxon	We're holding a sort of Industrial Seminar: a one-day event. It'll be here (Bristol Road, Birmingham). It's on "Telecoms in the Nineties", and I wondered if you'd like to give a talk.
Professor	Very kind. Yes - I could, in principle. What's the date?
Moxon	September 3rd. It's a nice day - good lunch, dinner, if you can stay. We could book you in somewhere.
Professor	Yes, I'd like to. If you could do all that, fine! What would you like me to talk about?
Moxon	I'd thought about international subscriber dialling and its applications.
Professor	That's no problem. What - an hour? Hour and a half?
Moxon	An hour, plus questions? Say, 11.30, to lunch at 1pm?
Professor	I'll have some slides to show. Maybe a video would be handy too.
Moxon	No problem. Anything else?
Professor	Do you need a text or a summary, or something, for the audience?
Moxon	Could you do a summary (a page or so)?
Professor	Yes. Do you want that in advance?
Moxon	If you could; at least a week really. For copying.
Professor	Thanks. Is there, er ....
Moxon	There's a fee. We're paying £200 to each speaker, plus all expenses, of course.
Professor	OK, that's fine. Mr Moxon, could I ask you to drop me a line to confirm what we've said, just so there's no misunderstanding?
Moxon	Sure. Well, I think that's everything for the moment. Many thanks again. We'll be in touch shortly.
Professor	My thanks to you. Bye bye.

Write an internal memo to Susan Emmett, the Seminar Support Organiser in RCB, asking her to make the arrangements.

(Series 4, 1990, Q4)

Now complete the following stages.

Stage 1: Identify the Task

....

Stage 2: Layout

To: ....

From: ....

Subject: ....

Date: ....

Stage 3: Identify Relevant Information

....

....

....

....

....

....

....

....

....

....

....

....

Stage 4: Group/Order Relevant Information

....

....

....

....

....

....

....

....

....

....

....

....

Stage 5: Write the Memo

Stage 6: Check your Work ☑

Checklist: Memo

1	Have you completed the task?	☐
2	Is it to the correct person? Is it from the correct person?	☐
3	Does the subject line tell you in a few words what the memo is about?	☐
4	Is it the correct date?	☐
5	Have you included all relevant information?	☐
6	Have you left out all irrelevant information?	☐
7	Have you ordered the information in the best way?	☐
8	Is the language appropriate for a memo?	☐
9	Have you checked spelling, grammar and punctuation?	☐

SECTION 4

Practice 8

You are the Personal Assistant of Mr O Dexter, Production Director of Vasta Products International Inc. He is on a business trip to the group factories in Europe, and had just telephoned you back at the office. Here are the notes you made:

Quality problems in Spain. Get Jo Hammond from Quality Assurance Department here asap. Also Bill Zetters. Need 3 - 4 days: moulding machine no good. So can't make London meeting with Kasser Bank (Peter Humphreys) on 18th. Suggest 23rd, same time, or later. Sorry. If no good, next trip! Or Sue Ferrentillo can go, 18th. Get a quick answer. Tell Jo H to ring Manuel (Madrid 259 3786) - technical questions.

Quick! Don't forget to explain why to Humphreys.

Write an internal memo to put on the desk of Jo Hammond when he returns from lunch.

(Series 3, 1990, Q4)

Now complete the following stages.

Stage 1:   Identify the Task

....

....

....

Stage 2:   Layout

To: ....

From: ....

Subject: ....

Date: ....

Stage 3:   Identify Relevant Information

....

....

....

....

....

....

....

....

....

....

....

Stage 4:   Group/Order Relevant Information

....

....

....

....

....

....

....

....

....

....

....

Stage 5: Write the Memo

Stage 6: Check your Work ☑

Checklist: Memo

1	Have you completed the task?	☐
2	Is it to the correct person? Is it from the correct person?	☐
3	Does the subject line tell you in a few words what the memo is about?	☐
4	Is it the correct date?	☐
5	Have you included all relevant information?	☐
6	Have you left out all irrelevant information?	☐
7	Have you ordered the information in the best way?	☐
8	Is the language appropriate for a memo?	☐
9	Have you checked spelling, grammar and punctuation?	☐

Practice 9

Today is the 16th March, you are the Sales Manager of a small manufacturing company. A customer, J Laval Ltd, has just telephoned with an urgent order and, after checking your production, you have made the following notes on the order form.

Telephone Orders

Customer	Product	Quantity	Order Date	Delivery Date	Internal Notes
J Laval Ltd	87A	1,000	16.3	23.3	OK
	88A	2,000	16.3	30.3	1,000 OK. Rest by 6 April.
	89A	500	16.3	17.3	Can't! No stock! 15th April earliest.

Please confirm delivery dates by telex.

Now send an internal memo to Peter Clough, the Production Manager, explaining the situation and asking him to give production priority to the appropriate products. You know that he will not be very happy to do so!

(Series 2, 1990, Q4)

Now complete the following stages.

Stage 1:   Identify the Task

....

Stage 2:   Layout

To: ....

From: ....

Subject: ....

Date: ....

Stage 3: Identify Relevant Information

....
....
....
....
....
....
....
....
....
....
....
....
....
....

Stage 4: Group/Order Relevant Information

....
....
....
....
....
....
....
....
....
....
....
....
....
....
....
....

Stage 5: Write the Memo

Stage 6: Check your Work ☑

Checklist: Memo

1	Have you completed the task?	☐
2	Is it to the correct person? Is it from the correct person?	☐
3	Does the subject line tell you in a few words what the memo is about?	☐
4	Is it the correct date?	☐
5	Have you included all relevant information?	☐
6	Have you left out all irrelevant information?	☐
7	Have you ordered the information in the best way?	☐
8	Is the language appropriate for a memo?	☐
9	Have you checked spelling, grammar and punctuation?	☐

Practice 10

John Llewellyn is a clerical assistant employed by Welshpool Welshcakes Ltd of Welshpool, Wales, SY1 4BN. In order to get his work done, John often works late unsupervised. He claims overtime for working late.

> John is seen coming home from work one evening at 6pm by his Personnel Officer. Next day, the Personnel Officer, who checks overtime claims, finds that John had claimed to be working until 7pm the previous night. The Personnel Officer then writes to John indicating why he must refuse payment and asks John to come and see him in his office the next day.

Task: Write the memorandum from the Personnel Officer to John.

(Series 3, 1993, Q4)

Now complete the following stages.

Stage 1: Identify the Task

....

Stage 2: Layout

To: ....

From: ....

Subject: ....

Date: ....

Stage 3: Identify Relevant Information

....

....

....

....

....

....

....

....

....

....

....

....

Stage 4: Group/Order Relevant Information

....

....

....

....

....

....

....

....

....

....

....

....

Stage 5: Write the Memo

Stage 6: Check your Work ☑

Checklist: Memo

1	Have you completed the task?	☐
2	Is it to the correct person? Is it from the correct person?	☐
3	Does the subject line tell you in a few words what the memo is about?	☐
4	Is it the correct date?	☐
5	Have you included all relevant information?	☐
6	Have you left out all irrelevant information?	☐
7	Have you ordered the information in the best way?	☐
8	Is the language appropriate for a memo?	☐
9	Have you checked spelling, grammar and punctuation?	☐

SECTION 5:   Miscellaneous

Introduction

Question 4, according to the Chief Examiner, is "A conversion task: you receive information input in one form - for example, a telex, or letter, or message - and you have to use this information to provide two other forms of communication: a memo, a letter, a telex, a facsimile or whatever." This question is worth 25 points for both answers and so each answer should be about half the length of answers for questions 1, 2 and 3. In this section the different tasks are considered. Memos have already been looked at in section 4.

Stage 1:   Identify the Task

Read the question carefully and work out exactly what you are required to do. Examples of instructions are "Draft notes" or "Draft a telex" or "Send a message by the most appropriate means" etc.

Stage 2:   Layout

As different tasks are required, appropriate layout must be used. The following provide some guidelines:

1   Notes need a subject and a date. Sentences are short and to the point.

2   A telex needs a telex number for the addressee, a telex number of the sender, time, date, an attention line (Attn) and your name and address at the bottom. You may be required to make up information such as time and telex numbers.

3   A notice needs a clear heading at the top. It must have the name and position of the person who wrote it at the bottom. It must also have a date at the bottom.

4   Messages for notice board display should have a title at the top and a signature, position and date at the bottom.

5   A code of good practice is a guideline or list informing people of what they should do. It should have a title, an introductory sentence and have a name and date at the bottom. Numbered points are useful.

6   A description is a piece of text divided into paragraphs for different themes. A title is useful.

7   A summary is a piece of text. You may use numbered points but these are not always necessary.

8   A fax (facsimile) requires the headings: to, from, date and number of pages including this one.

9   A list needs a title and numbered points.

If you are asked to send a message by the most appropriate means, make it clear which means you have chosen and use appropriate layout.

Stage 3:   Identify Relevant Information

This will depend on the task. Work out what information is needed to complete the task. Information is relevant if the message is not complete without it.

Stage 4:   Group/Order Relevant Information

Often the information in the question is presented in a suitable order. Sometimes, however, the different information may be mixed up. Make sure you group things logically and order them suitably.

Stage 5:   Write the Answer

Language is short and to the point in notes, lists, notices and faxes. Telexes use short sentences often leaving out the subject, prepositions, articles (eg Arrive 10am Tuesday). Descriptions and summaries use longer flowing sentences as they are continuous text.

Stage 6:   Check your Work

Checklist: Miscellaneous

The following is a list of points to check.

1   Have you completed the task?
2   Is the layout you have chosen appropriate for the task?
3   Is the information relevant?
4   Is the information in the right order?
5   Is the language appropriate?
6   Have you checked grammar, spelling and punctuation?

SECTION 5

Practice 1

You work for Owen Construction plc of Vauxhall Bridge Road, London SW14 4AJ, as a committee clerk. Owing to an outbreak of influenza at your firm, you have to postpone a meeting of your firm's representatives with representatives of local government, estate agents, solicitors and other firms concerned with the possible relocation of your firm to the Docklands area of London.

Eventually you are able to reconvene the meeting at Vauxhall Bridge Road, moving the date from the original Friday 9 September at 2pm to Monday 26 September at 10am.

Task: Draft notes for your secretary to use when phoning those scheduled to attend the meeting. The notes should indicate changes made, including a reminder of the earlier start, and that food would be available at lunchtime. Indicate in your notes that all delegates would need to be advised of the changes.

(Series 2, 1992, Q4)

Stage 1: Identify the Task
Draft notes.

Stage 2: Layout
Notes need a subject and a date. They use short sentences and are to the point.

Subject: Rearranged date for meeting concerning possible relocation to Docklands.

Date: 2nd September 1992

Stage 3: Identify Relevant Information
- influenza outbreak
- meeting postponed
- reconvene meeting
- Vauxhall Bridge Road
- old date was Friday 9th September at 2pm
- new date is Monday 26th September at 10am
- lunch available
- advise delegates of changes

Stage 4: Group/Order Relevant Information
1   Outbreak of influenza.
2   Caused meeting on Friday 9th September to be cancelled.
3   Reconvened on Monday 26th September at 10am, Vauxhall Bridge Road.
4   Advise all delegates of changes.
5   Remind them of earlier start.
6   Lunch will be available.

Stage 5: Write the Answer

Subject: Rearranged date for meeting concerning possible relocation to Docklands.

Date: 2nd September 1992

Outbreak of influenza at our company has caused the meeting originally planned for Friday 9th September at 2pm to be cancelled. The meeting will be reconvened at Vauxhall Bridge Road on Monday 26 September at 10am.

Advise all delegates of the changes. Don't forget to mention the changes, especially of the earlier start and point out that food will be available at lunch time.

Stage 6:   Check your Work

Checklist: Miscellaneous

1	Have you completed the task?	☑
2	Is the layout you have chosen appropriate for the task?	☑
3	Is the information relevant?	☑
4	Is the information in the right order?	☑
5	Is the language appropriate?	☑
6	Have you checked spelling, grammar and punctuation?	☑

SECTION 5

Practice 2

Your firm Monroe Electronics has a factory near the sea in a low lying part of East Anglia. After a particularly rainy spell of weather you receive an advance warning from a nearby weather station that heavy flooding is expected, beginning in about twelve hours' time and lasting for several days. As Managing Director of the firm you are faced with a number of decisions.

To his secretary, the MD says, "I want to send some circular letters. I think we should send them to our customers and our suppliers, but I'll draft the one for customers first. Then I'll give you some notes so you can compose a staff message for notice board display."

"I think our customers should be told that we have a temporary crisis on our hands and how long it will last is uncertain. Let them know that we will definitely try to maintain deliveries. But obviously point out to them that we do not know whether many programmed deliveries will be late and how long our present supply of products will last. That is especially true if our suppliers cannot get through to us. Make sure that they understand we are still succeeding in business and it is just fate that is making us do this. Nobody will be happier than us when the situation returns to normal."

"The message to staff should include the following: All non-essential staff should remain at home for three days (they should check with their department heads to see if they're non-essential). They should check by phone, on the third day that they can return to work next day. Warn them that they may not get through on the phone straightaway. Staff will be on half pay for the days they're not in."

"Essential staff should attempt to keep working at the firm. Advise them that our success in this time of disaster will benefit their future".

Task: Draft a message for all employees for notice board display.

(Series 1, 1992, Q4)

Stage 1:   Identify the Task

Draft a message for all employees for notice board display.

Stage 2:   Layout

This is for notice board display so should have a title at the top and a signature, position and date at the bottom.

Stage 3:   Identify Relevant Information

- non-essential staff to stay at home for 3 days
- check with heads of the departments if they are non-essential
- check by phone on day 3 if they can return
- may take time to get through
- half pay on days when they do not come in
- essential staff to keep on working
- have to get through this crisis
- success now good for future

Stage 4:   Group/Order Relevant Information

1   Check with Heads of Departments to see if they are essential or non-essential staff.

2   Non-essential staff to:
- stay at home for 3 days
- check on day 3 if they can return
- may take time to get through
- half pay on those days they do not come in

3   Essential staff to keep on working.

4   We have to get through this crisis. Success now is good for our future.

Stage 5:   Write the Answer

Procedure During Floods

All staff must check with the Head of their Department if they are essential or non-essential staff.

Non-essential staff are to:

•   stay at home for 3 days
•   check on day 3 if they can return.

It may take some time to get through, please do not give up.

During this period non-essential staff will receive half pay on the days which they do not come in.

Essential staff are to keep on working.

We have to get through this crisis and success now will benefit our common future.

Jack Smith

Jack Smith
Managing Director
10th March 1992

Now complete the following stage.

Stage 6:   Check your Work   ☑

Checklist: Miscellaneous

1	Have you completed the task?	☐
2	Is the layout you have chosen appropriate for the task?	☐
3	Is the information relevant?	☐
4	Is the information in the right order?	☐
5	Is the language appropriate?	☐
6	Have you checked spelling, grammar and punctuation?	☐

Practice 3

You are the Personal Assistant of Mr O Dexter, Production Director of Vasta Products International Inc. He is on a business trip to the group factories in Europe, and has just telephoned you back at the office. Here are the notes you made:

Quality problems in Spain. Get Jo Hammond from Quality Assurance Department here asap. Also Bill Zetters. Need 3 - 4 days: moulding machine no good. So can't make London meeting with Kasser Bank (Peter Humphreys) on 18th. Suggest 23rd, same time, or later. Sorry. If no good, next trip! Or Sue Ferrentillo can go, 18th. Get a quick answer. Tell Jo H to ring Manuel (Madrid 259 3786) - technical questions. Quick!

Don't forget to explain why to Humphreys.

Task: Draft the telex to Peter Humphreys at Kasser Bank.

(Series 3, 1990, Q4)

Stage 1: Identify the Task

Draft a telex.

Stage 2: Layout

Addressee's telex number:	12347 Kasser Bank
Sender's telex number:	89321 Vasta Products International Inc
Time:	12.21
Date:	16th July 1990
Attention line:	Peter Humphreys
Complimentary close:	Best regards
Name and position:	(your name), PA
	Vasta Products International Inc
	Basingstoke, Hampshire, EE4 6ZJ

Stage 3: Identify Relevant Information

- problems come up in Spain
- Mr Dexter on a business trip
- to group factories in Europe
- can't make meeting
- Kasser Bank - Peter Humphreys
- on 18th
- suggest on 23rd at same time or later
- apologies
- if not possible then wait till next trip
- or Sue Ferrentillo can go
- need quick reply

Stage 4: Group/Order Relevant Information

1. Problems come up in Spain.
2. Mr Dexter on a business trip.
3. To group factories in Europe.
4. Can't make meeting.
5. Kasser Bank.
6. Peter Humphreys.
7. On 18th.
8. Suggest on 23rd at same time or later.
9. Apologies.
10. If not possible then wait till next trip.
11. Or Sue Ferrentillo can go.
12. Need quick reply.

Now complete the following stages.

Stage 5: Write the Answer

Stage 6: Check your Work ✓

Checklist: Miscellaneous

1   Have you completed the task?   ☐
2   Is the layout you have chosen appropriate for the task?   ☐
3   Is the information relevant?   ☐
4   Is the information in the right order?   ☐
5   Is the language appropriate?   ☐
6   Have you checked spelling, grammar and punctuation?   ☐

Practice 4

Below is the transcript of a conversation between Senior Personnel Officer, James Henry, and his Labour Officer, Peter Jones. Both are employed by the nylon spinning firm of Henry Morgan Ltd of Pontypridd in South Wales.

JH	I still can't understand how so many people can be so late so often.
PJ	Well I think more of our staff live further away from the plant than they used to - and the women who have children may be delayed or even absent on occasion. We do employ a lot more women than we used to.
JH	Yes, and of course, those cuts in public bus services don't help. Perhaps we should try to get additional bus services for our workers. I can't see how the buses couldn't make a profit. Of course another alternative is to provide our own bus or even charter one.
PJ	It wouldn't matter so much if the railways up the valley could be relied upon - but trains are often cancelled or delayed. Of course there is also the possibility that many of our workers - especially the part timers - find the work very monotonous. I often wonder if we couldn't improve things in the production area to keep the workers happy.
JH	I think all the points mentioned have credibility. I think a wise move would be to consult the Work's Union convenor, Jimmy Smythe, to see what he thinks. He may be able to suggest a number of ideas; though I'm not sure if he'll want to support the part timers very much. Many of them are not interested in the Union.

Task: Draft a summary of the problems facing Henry Morgan Ltd.

(Series 1, 1993, Q4)

Stage 1: Identify the Task
Draft a summary of the problems facing Henry Morgan Ltd.

Stage 2: Layout
A summary is continuous text. You may use numbered points but these are not always necessary.

Stage 3: Identify Relevant Information	Stage 4: Group/Order Relevant Information
- people coming late	....
- living further away	....
- cuts in public transport	....
- regular cancellations of trains	....
- women delayed	....
- monotonous work	....

Stage 5: Write the Answer

Stage 6: Check your Work

Checklist: Miscellaneous

1	Have you completed the task?	☐
2	Is the layout you have chosen appropriate for the task?	☐
3	Is the information relevant?	☐
4	Is the information in the right order?	☐
5	Is the language appropriate?	☐
6	Have you checked spelling, grammar and punctuation?	☐

Practice 5

You are the Safety Officer of SH Gruber, stove manufacturers of the Wirral Trading Estate, Brikenhead, Cheshire, BN13 4SJ. A serious accident is reported to you - a machinist has lost his left hand in an accident in the production shop. You visit the production shop and say to yourself:

> The machine is very poorly maintained, too much grease and not enough in the right places. Protecting cover for the arms and face appears to have been removed. Oil around the machine and on the floor. It's a good job there are no H & S Inspectors around.

You talk to the foreman: (S = self / F = foremen)

S	"What was Hopkins, the machinist wearing?"
F	"Gloves."
S	'That's all right. Hasn't he got long hair?"
F	"Yes, it was tied up in an elastic band."
S	(*Thinks*) I don't believe it. Now I recall he's also been for eye tests recently.
S	"Had he been drinking?"
F	"Probably had a couple at lunch time!"
S	"Incredible! He knows these machines must be operated with extreme caution!"

Afterwards, your suggestions include: arranging a meeting for all production staff, ensuring the Health and Safety Acts are posted everywhere; that company requirements for safety are known to all; and making sure that nobody is stupid enough to flout regulations whilst wearing inappropriate dress or hair styles.

Task: Draft a **notice** to be displayed in various parts of your premises warning of the hazards of using machines incorrectly.

(Series 1, 1991, Q4)

Stage 1:   Identify the Task

Draft a notice.

Stage 2:   Layout

A notice requires a clear heading at the top. It must have the name and position of the person who wrote it at the bottom. It must also have a date at the bottom.

Stage 3:   Identify Relevant Information

....

....

....

....

....

....

Stage 4:   Group/Order Relevant Information

....

....

....

....

....

....

Stage 5: Write the Answer

Stage 6: Check your Work

Checklist: Miscellaneous

1   Have you completed the task? ☐
2   Is the layout you have chosen appropriate for the task? ☐
3   Is the information relevant? ☐
4   Is the information in the right order? ☐
5   Is the language appropriate? ☐
6   Have you checked spelling, grammar and punctuation? ☐

Practice 6

As assistant to the Managing Director of Grow Foods plc, a food production firm of Afton Vale, Hereford, you receive a telephone call one morning from an official at Buckingham Palace. The call confirms that a Prince of the Royal Family will be visiting the firm on a Thursday in two months' time. You are asked to make arrangements for a visit lasting one and a half hours beginning at 11 am on the day (the Prince has another earlier engagement in the vicinity) and "Yes, the royal personage would be happy to spend half an hour of his time at the firm at a buffet lunch with directors at 12 noon but would have to be away promptly at 12.30 pm for another engagement in a town twenty five miles away. Formal acceptance of his visit will follow shortly."

Your superior is delighted and says "Better get ourselves organised and call a meeting of all the senior managers for Friday next, 15th July. We'll have to tell them to make sure that everything is neat and tidy in all departments on the day; that everyone in the offices comes looking well-dressed and that canteen staff, production shop and transport workers are kept informed and advised of the great honour being done our firm by this visit. Could be a good idea to call meetings of those four areas separately - canteen, offices, production shop and transport - to advise on how the possible disruption of the visit could affect them. Can you see to these points please? I'll let the directors know."

Task: **Prepare notes** for the MD in his talk to Canteen Staff. Include in your notes a few reminders that cleanliness in dress and equipment is essential and that staff should be alert to respond to situations quickly on the day. You naturally add comments about the honour to the firm, the date and timing of the event - and other points considered significant.

(Series 3, 1992, Q4)

Stage 1: Identify the Task

Prepare notes.

Now complete the following stages.

Stage 2: Layout

....

....

Stage 3: Identify Relevant Information

....

....

....

....

....

....

....

....

....

Stage 4: Group/Order Relevant Information

....

....

....

....

....

....

....

....

....

Stage 5: Write the Answer

Stage 6: Check your Work

Checklist: Miscellaneous

1	Have you completed the task?	☐
2	Is the layout you have chosen appropriate for the task?	☐
3	Is the information relevant?	☐
4	Is the information in the right order?	☐
5	Is the language appropriate?	☐
6	Have you checked spelling, grammar and punctuation?	☐

Practice 7

John Walker, the Managing Director of Elsom Export plc, of Birmingham, is angry and disconsolate. He declares with some vehemence:

"This company is losing a lot of money when our sales reps go into Europe. I've just had a report from our insurers; they intend to raise our insurance premiums for overseas travel because our reps in Europe are making too much use of private medical facilities for minor ailments - and these are very costly. They should be using state medical services for minor matters when in EEC countries, all they need is From E111. They must abide by the same system we offer them at home; private medical care for major health problems and the National Health Service for coughs and colds. It might be a good idea too for them to check what they need in the way of injections and medicines in other countries when they're about to go away.

Another thing is that too many of our reps are changing English money abroad anywhere they happen to be. This is expensive and wasteful. We have facilities here for arranging foreign currency. Why aren't they using travellers' cheques (we provide them) and credit cards? They're safer than cash. Tell them too, that if they don't stop these wasteful ways, heads will roll. Job losses will soon cure them!"

As your Managing Director's PA, you listen to this tirade and then tackle the following task.

Task: **Draw up a Code of Good Practice** for when your firm's representatives begin to plan trips abroad.

(Series 2, 1991, Q4)

Now complete the following stages.

Stage 1: Identify the Task

....

Stage 2: Layout

....

....

Stage 3: Identify Relevant Information	**Stage 4: Group/Order Relevant Information**
....	....
....	....
....	....
....	....
....	....
....	....
....	....
....	....
....	....

Stage 5: Write the Answer

Stage 6: Check your Work

Checklist: Miscellaneous

1	Have you completed the task?	☐
2	Is the layout you have chosen appropriate for the task?	☐
3	Is the information relevant?	☐
4	Is the information in the right order?	☐
5	Is the language appropriate?	☐
6	Have you checked spelling, grammar and punctuation?	☐

SECTION 5

Practice 8

You are the assistant to the Managing Director of a multi national company based in Liverpool. Prior to his going on holiday, your Managing Director asks you, his personal assistant, to arrange accommodation for the sales representatives, of the European branches of your company, who will be attending a conference in Lausanne, Switzerland.

The conference that your company - Lewis, Bruhl & Co - will be holding is to last for four days from 21st February 1993. At the last count, thirty four staff had indicated they would attend - later submissions could raise this to forty.

You contact the Hotel du Lac in Lausanne asking them for single bedrooms for all those likely to attend and indicating you would like full board for the duration of the conference and for full conference facilities to be available.

Task: **Draft a fax** for transmission to all your European branches confirming the conference and the reservation of accommodation. Indicate that two representatives of the same sex may be asked to share a room.

(Series 2, 1993, Q4)

Now complete the following stages.

Stage 1: Identify the Task

....

Stage 2: Layout

....

....

Stage 3: Identify Relevant Information	Stage 4: Group/Order Relevant Information
....	....
....	....
....	....
....	....
....	....
....	....
....	....
....	....
....	....

Stage 5: Write the Answer

Stage 6: Check your Work

Checklist: Miscellaneous

1	Have you completed the task?	☐
2	Is the layout you have chosen appropriate for the task?	☐
3	Is the information relevant?	☐
4	Is the information in the right order?	☐
5	Is the language appropriate?	☐
6	Have you checked spelling, grammar and punctuation?	☐

SECTION 5

Practice 9

You are the personal assistant to Mr Henry Wilson who is the "troubleshooter" for the Western Petroleum Company which is based at Grampian Street, Aberdeen, Scotland. Shortly Mr Wilson is to visit Norway to discuss possible cooperation on oil rig safety measures in the North Sea oil fields. He disappears, leaving you with the following message.

> Send an urgent message to Mr Ove Berenson of Norge-Fisk AB, Bergen, Norway, indicating that I'll be arriving in Bergen around 11am, I think, two days from now. Check my flight details. Request I'm met (it always rains in Bergen!) Would like an early meeting (must make full use of my time) preferably during the afternoon of my arrival. Essential that I meet all personnel involved whilst I'm there - must, repeat **must**, receive all relevant data - there's no second chance with safety!

Task: Send the message - by the most appropriate means. (Indicate the means chosen.)

(Series 4, 1992, Q4)

Now complete the following stages.

Stage 1: Identify the Task

....

Stage 2: Layout

....

....

Stage 3: Identify Relevant Information

....

....

....

....

....

....

....

....

....

Stage 4: Group/Order Relevant Information

....

....

....

....

....

....

....

....

....

Stage 5: Write the Answer

Stage 6: Check your Work ☑

Checklist: Miscellaneous

1	Have you completed the task?	☐
2	Is the layout you have chosen appropriate for the task?	☐
3	Is the information relevant?	☐
4	Is the information in the right order?	☐
5	Is the language appropriate?	☐
6	Have you checked spelling, grammar and punctuation?	☐

Practice 10

The following is a conversation between the Advertising Manager, Mr James Attridge, and one of his assistants, Miss Petra Angelis, in the firm of Attridge and Barnaby, advertising agents.

JA   "Morning Petra. Any ideas yet about the project for Pearlsons' soap advertising campaign?"

PA   "I've had a few - some of them unworkable. But there is an idea I'd like to try."

JA   "Well what is it - how much does it cost? I think the logistics are important to work out."

PA   "Oh, I agree. So what I'd like to do is to use that well tried formula of consumer testing. You know - like the ones where you test the use of a commodity and prove by various means that ours is the best. It's been tried to test the taste of margarine too."

JA   "Yes, I see..., but if it's been tried before, isn't it a bit old hat and won't people think we're just jumping on the bandwagon?

PA   "To some extent, but I thought we could go beyond that. After the consumer testing, we could actually take the consumers and show them precisely how the soap is made, how it is developed - and so on. This might be a step ahead of those companies who just show the consumers being very pleased with the soap. We could present our adverts in two parts. Perhaps they could be a little longer than usual but when people get used to our presentations on TV and elsewhere, we could show either part of the advertisement - separately - rather like that marvellous dog food advert which sometimes shows a part or whole sequence of the dogs scampering across moorland. In time people would be aware of the whole sequence. If past efforts of a similar nature are anything to go by, sales should soar.

JA   "Right - let's plan it in detail."

Task: Write a description of the proposed project for the file.

(Series 4, 1991, Q4)

Now complete the following stages.

Stage 1: Identify the Task

....

Stage 2: Layout

....

....

Stage 3: Identify Relevant Information

....

....

....

....

....

....

....

....

....

....

....

....

Stage 4: Group/Order Relevant Information

....

....

....

....

....

....

....

....

....

....

....

....

Stage 5: Write the Answer

Stage 6: Check your Work ☑

Checklist: Miscellaneous

1	Have you completed the task?	☐
2	Is the layout you have chosen appropriate for the task?	☐
3	Is the information relevant?	☐
4	Is the information in the right order?	☐
5	Is the language appropriate?	☐
6	Have you checked spelling, grammar and punctuation?	☐

ANSWER KEY

Practice 3

Stage 5: Write the Letter

13 Doncaster Road
Sheffield
South Yorks
S1 4AH

(today's date)

Swaythings Ltd
Tadcaster
Yorks
TA1 3AJ

Dear Sirs

Meat pie bought in Easterly Supermarket

Last week I bought one of your meat pies from Easterly's Supermarket in Sheffield. When I was eating the pie for my lunch, I suddenly bit into something hard and there was a loud crack. I carefully removed the bits of pie from my mouth and two teeth which I had recently had capped came out with them.

Only the week before I had paid £200 for my dentist to cap these teeth. I was furious, especially when I realised that what I had bitten into was a half inch piece of metal. Imagine what may have happened if I had swallowed it.

I enclose the wrapper, showing where I bought the pie, and also the piece of metal. I intend to take this matter further and my solicitor is at present looking into a variety of Health and Safety Acts, Consumer Protection Acts and a number of Acts of Parliament where we can take action.

I expect to receive an apology from you, immediate compensation for the damage done and your view on this matter.

Yours faithfully

Alec Paxton

Alec Paxton

Practice 4

Stage 4: Group/Order Relevant Information

1 Answered advertisement in the "Norwich Newsman".

2 Rented cabin cruiser for 2 weeks to tour Norfolk Broads.

3 Booking number 367/4A.

4 Travelled all day from Barrow.

5 Arrived at Oulton Broad to collect boat.

6 Found: - boat half in water
  - was only half the size promised
  - only two bunks - no sleeping accommodation for children
  - no provision on board as promised
  - nothing on which to cook or heat any food
  - bathroom and toilet a joke

7 Contacted your representative Mr S Williams.

8 Most unhelpful, quote "It is your problem."

9 Family, especially children, had been looking forward to holiday.

10 Holiday ruined because of broken promises.

11 Money back plus compensation.

12 Broadcast the situation on BBC and ITV travel programmes.

13 Hope to receive prompt reply and settlement.

14 If not expect to hear from my solicitor.

Stage 5: Write the Letter

3 Workington Way
Barrow
Lancashire   BA4 4NK

(today's date)

Cruising for Pleasure
Oulton Broad
Norfolk   LO3 4NJ

Dear Sirs

Cabin cruiser rented at Oulton Broad

Some weeks ago, after answering an advertisement in the "Norwich Newsman" I rented a cabin cruiser for two weeks to tour the Norfolk Broads (booking number 367/4A). After travelling all day by train from Barrow in Lancashire, we arrived at Oulton Broad to collect the boat and found:

- the boat was half in the water
- it was only half the size promised
- there were only two bunks and no sleeping accommodation for the children
- there were no provisions on the boat as promised
- there was nothing on which to cook or heat any food and the bathroom and toilet were a joke!

We immediately contacted your representative, Mr S Williams, who was most unhelpful, and told us it was our problem.

My whole family had been looking forward to this holiday, especially the children, but the holiday was ruined because of broken promises made by your company. The very least you can do is repay the money we paid you for the holiday, plus some form of compensation. If not then I will make sure that this whole situation is broadcast on both the BBC and ITV travel programmes. I'm sure they will be only too pleased to inform the public of the state of your boats and of the way you keep your promises.

I hope to receive a prompt reply and settlement. If not, you can expect to be hearing from my solicitor in the next few days.

Yours faithfully

John Farmer

John Farmer

Practice 5

Stage 3: Identify Relevant Information

- received letter of complaint from Miss Murray
- investigated the matter
- fruit pies past their sell-by date
- spoke to Manager of Wateron's Bridgwater
- assured fruit pies either sold before sell-by date or removed from shelves
- very careful about this/perishable goods checked regularly
- no liability because past sell-by date
- no explanation as to how this could have happened
- however, quality of goods/customer service very important
- replace packet of fruit pies
- check sell-by dates in future before you buy goods
- inform Manager if goods are past sell-by date

Stage 4: Group/Order Relevant Information

1   Received letter of complaint.
2   Examined packet, pies four weeks past sell-by date.
3   Therefore no liability on our part.
4   Investigated matter carefully.
5   Spoke to Manager of Wateron's.
6   Assured us pies either sold before sell-by date or removed from shelves.
7   Are very careful about this.
8   Perishable goods checked regularly.
9   No explanation how this could have happened.
10 Doubt pies could have been bought on date stated.
11 However, quality of goods and customer satisfaction vital.
12 Replace packet of fruit pies.
13 Check sell-by dates in future before buying.
14 Inform Shop Manager at once if goods are past sell-by date.

ANSWER KEY

Stage 5: Write the Letter

Complaints Department
Ashill Food Products plc
Unit 5
Wolsey Estate
Ashill
Somerset
TN5 8DG

(today's date)

Miss Murray
36 Langport Road
Zoyland
Bridgwater
Somerset
TN15 9VX

Dear Miss Murray

Damaged Fruit Pies

We have received your letter complaining about the packet of fruit pies you bought which were in bad condition. On examining the packet you enclosed, we noticed the pies were over 4 weeks past their sell-by date and therefore by law we bear no liability for these goods.

We have investigated the matter carefully and have spoken to the Manager of Wateron's Supermarket in Bridgwater. He assured us that fruit pies, as with other goods, are either sold before their sell-by date or removed from the shelves. He is very careful about this and all perishable goods are checked regularly.

We have given this matter careful thought and can find no explanation as to how a packet of fruit pies - four weeks past their sell-by date - could have been bought on the day you said.

However, the quality of our products and customer satisfaction are of vital importance to us and we shall therefore be sending you, under separate cover, a packet of fruit pies to replace the ones which were damaged. I would ask you though, in future, to check the sell-by dates of products before buying the goods and if you find that goods have gone past their sell-by dates, to inform the Manager immediately.

Yours sincerely

pp (your signature)
(Supervisor's name)
Supervisor, Complaints Department

Practice 6

Stage 2: Layout

- your address - MacDonald Component Parts Ltd, Halesowen, Birmingham, B9 5PQ
- addressee - Company Secretary, Parker Brown Ltd, 5 Dukinfield Square, Manchester M3 2JY
- date - (today's date)
- salutation - Dear Sir/Madam - in this text, although we have been given a name, we do not know the sex of G Saunders
- close - Yours faithfully
- subject line - Extension of payment
- signature - your signature
  name - your name
  position - Accounts Manager

Stage 3: Identify Relevant Information

- ref letter requesting to pay bill later

- asking for £3,000 more credit

- no extra credit

- 2 months extension at the most

Stage 4: Group/Order Relevant Information

1 Acknowledge receipt of letter asking for extension on overdue balance.
2 Note request for extra £3,000 credit.
3 Careful consideration/prepared to grant 2 months extension.
4 Appreciate difficulties but cannot allow any extra credit at present.

Stage 5: Write the Letter

MacDonald Component Parts Ltd
Halesowen
Birmingham   B9 5PQ

(today's date)

Company Secretary
Parker Brown Ltd
5 Dukinfield Square
Manchester   M3 2JY

Dear Sir/Madam

Extension of Payment

We acknowledge receipt of your letter asking for an extension of payment on your overdue balance. We note also your request for an extra £3,000 credit.

After careful consideration of your letter, we are prepared to grant you an extension of two months on your account. However, although we appreciate your difficulties, we cannot allow any extra credit at the present time.

Yours faithfully

(your signature)
(your name)
Accounts Manager

ANSWER KEY

Practice 7

Stage 1: Identify the Task
Write a letter.

Stage 2: Layout
*   your address - New Sounds, Unit 4, Shelton Industrial Estate, Holbarn, Manchester, M60 1AZ
*   addressee - Mr Murphy, O'Connel's Records, 97 Liffey Road, Dublin 9, Eire
*   date - 15th April 1991
*   salutation - Dear Mr Murphy
*   close - Your sincerely
*   subject line - Incorrect consignment
*   signature   -   your signature
    name   -   your name
    position   -   Marketing Manager

Stage 3: Identify Relevant Information
-   ref phone call of 15th April, re incorrect consignment
-   checked order with Sales Department
-   100 sets "New Moon" not ordered
-   100 sets "Night at the Greek" ordered
-   checked with Despatch Department
-   despatch of orders correct
-   Ref ARD/103 dated 03-04-91
-   will investigate further
-   possible mix up with shops or delivery service
-   apologies
-   will re-send order immediately

Stage 4: Group/Order Relevant Information
1   Ref phone call of 15th April, re incorrect consignment.
2   Checked order with Sales Department.
3   100 sets "New Moon" not ordered.
4   100 sets "Night at the Greek" ordered.
5   Checked with Despatch Department.
6   Despatch of orders correct.
7   Ref ARD/103 dated 03-04-91.
8   Will investigate further.
9   Possible mix up with shops or delivery service.
10   Apologies.
11   Will re-send order immediately.

Stage 5: Write the Letter

New Sounds
Unit 4
Shelton Industrial Estate
Holbarn
Manchester
M60 1AZ

15th April 1991

Mr Murphy
O'Connel's Records
97 Liffey Road
Dublin 9
Eire

Dear Mr Murphy

Incorrect Consignment

With reference to our phone call of this morning, concerning the incorrect consignment of goods you have received, I have checked with our Sales Department and according to our records you ordered 100 sets of "New Moon" and "Night at the Greek" and not 200 sets of "New Moon" and 100 sets of "Night at the Greek" as you stated in your phone call.

I have also checked with our Despatch Department and they confirm that your order Ref ARD/103 was despatched correctly on 3rd April 1991. I will look further into this matter but at the present moment can only assume there has been a mix up on the part of the delivery service and that you have received someone else's order.

I have arranged for your order to be put together and it will be despatched immediately.

Please accept my apologies and assurances that this will not happen again.

Yours sincerely

(your signature)
(your name)
Marketing Manager

ANSWER KEY

Practice 8

Stage 1: Identify the Task

Send a conciliatory letter.

Stage 2: Layout

- your address - Planet Travel Ltd, The Green, New Malden, Surrey, KT14 5SU
- addressee - Mr N Heilbrunn, Moreway Plastics Ltd, Strangeway Place, Sutton, SU23 1JK
- date - (today's date)
- salutation - Dear Mr Heilbrunn
- close - Yours sincerely
- subject line - Problems on recent business trip
- signature - your signature
  name   - your name
  position   - Assistant Manager

Stage 3: Identify Relevant Information

- sorry to hear about problems
- spoken to clerk
- looking into some of the specific points
- clerk reprimanded
- offer sincere apology
- assure that future itineraries will be arranged with more care and attention

Stage 4: Group/Order Relevant Information

1   Sorry to hear about problems on your recent business trip in southern Europe.
2   Have spoken to clerk concerned.
3   Has been reprimanded.
4   We are looking into some of the specific points.
5   Offer my sincere apologies.
6   Assure you that future travel itineraries will be arranged with more care and attention.

Stage 5: Write the Letter

Planet Travel Ltd
The Green
New Malden
Surrey   KT14 5SU

(today's date)

Mr N Heilbrunn
Moreway Plastics Ltd
Strangeway Place
Sutton   SU23 1JK

Dear Mr Heilbrunn

Problems on recent business trip

I was very sorry to hear about the problems you experienced on your recent business trip through southern Europe. I have spoken to the clerk who looked after your travel arrangements and he has been reprimanded.

We are looking into some of the specific points you mentioned. I can only offer my most sincere apologies and can assure you that your future travel itineraries will be arranged with more care and attention.

Yours sincerely

(your signature)
(your name)
Assistant Manager

Practice 9

Stage 1: Identify the Task

Write a letter.

Stage 2: Layout

- your address - Waterloo Station, London SE1
- addressee - Mr Williams, 17 The High Street, North Walsham, NR3 5AJ
- date - (today's date)
- salutation - Dear Mr Williams
- close - Yours sincerely
- subject line - Problems with travel information
- signature/name/position - your signature, your name, Station Master's Representative

Stage 3: Identify Relevant Information

- acknowledge receipt of letter
- BR divided into regions
- Anglia for Norwich
- SE for London and SE
- N Walsham to Bristol not SE
- direct complaint to BR Anglia region
- two parts
- punctuality - 3 mins late/miss train
- N Walsham facilities you should have known
- returning bill/cannot pay

Stage 4: Group/Order Relevant Information

1 Acknowledge receipt of letter.
2 Sympathise with regard to problems.
3 Journey from North Walsham to Bristol via London.
4 BR divided up into regions.
5 Anglia based in Norwich.
6 SE regions based at Waterloo.
7 Direct complaint to Norwich.
8 Necessary to take you up on one or two points.
9 Punctuality - if 3 mins late should expect to miss train.
10 Catering arrangements listed on timetables.
11 N Walsham facilities you should have known.
12 Returning bill, cannot pay it.

Stage 5: Write the Letter

Waterloo Station
London   SE1

(today's date)

Mr Williams
17 The High Street
North Walsham   NR3 5AJ

Dear Mr Williams

Problems with travel information

We acknowledge receipt of your letter and whilst sympathise with you with regard to the problems you experienced on your recent journey from North Walsham to Bristol via London, I must point out that, as I'm sure you know, British Rail is divided up into regions. The region you should be writing to is Anglia, based in Norwich. At Waterloo we are responsible for British Rail South East region. I would therefore suggest you direct your complaint to your local offices of British Rail in Norwich.

I do, however, feel it necessary to take you up on one or two points you mentioned. At British Rail we try to run a punctual service and if passengers arrive after the scheduled departure time they cannot expect to catch the train. With regard to catering arrangements, they are always listed on timetables and I would have thought if North Walsham is your local station you would have known when their facilities are open.

However, as already mentioned, the best thing is for you to direct your complaint to the Station Master at Norwich Station, British Rail Anglia Region. I return your bill as I'm sure you'll appreciate we cannot pay it.

Yours sincerely

(your signature)
(your name)
Station Master's Representative

Practice 10

Stage 1: Identify the Task

Write Fred Jones' letter.

Stage 2: Layout

- your address - The Kent Film Complex, High Street, South Cheriton, CT13 7AJ
- addressee - GB Eurofilm Company, Wardour Street, London, SW12 4AJ
- date - (today's date)
- salutation - Dear Sirs
- subject line - Delivery of film
- close - Yours faithfully
- signature -   signature
  name   -   Fred Jones
  position   -   Cinema Manager

Stage 3: Identify Relevant Information

- films 2 days overdue
- unheard of in cinema trade
- close cinema
- hold on to films for 2 more days
- show back-up films
- however has paid for advertising in advance for films now not showing
- possible legal action from cinema goers
- could lose clients
- very competitive business
- cannot afford to close cinema
- would make no money if showed existing films for 2 more days
- most cinema goers already seen them
- back-up films - attendance could fall drastically
- now on 3rd day overdue before films will be delivered in 2 more days
- flu "bug" has upset delivery schedules
- distributors should have more effective fail-safe system of delivery

Stage 4: Group/Order Relevant Information

1   Films delivered 2 days late.
2   Unheard of in cinema trade.
3   Now two more days delay.
4   Flu "bug" disrupted delivery schedules.
5   Advertising for 2 weeks not showing films/haven't been delivered.
6   Financial loss.
7   Legal action.
8   Could close down.
9   Loss of income/can't afford to.
10 Lose clients.
11 Very competitive business.
12 Could hold on to films we have - domino effect.
13 Most cinema goers already seen films.
14 Make no money showing them.
15 Showing back-up films out of necessity.
16 Attendance will not be high.
17 Distributor should have better fail-safe system of delivery before it is too late.

Stage 5:   Write the Letter

The Kent Film Complex
High Street
South Cheriton
CT13 7AJ

(today's date)

GB Eurofilm Company
Wardour Street
London
SW12 4AJ

Dear Sirs

<u>Delivery of Films</u>

Films that are delivered two days late is almost unheard of in the local cinema trade. Now you inform me that it will be two more days before the films can be delivered because a flu "bug" has severely disrupted your delivery schedule.

What about my schedules? I've been advertising for 2 weeks now for films I should be showing but cannot because they haven't been delivered yet. Quite apart from the financial loss incurred, I am also laying myself open to possible legal action from cinema goers. I could close down until the films arrive but I cannot afford to do this. Would you pay for my lost income? And what about the clients I would lose - this is as you know a very competitive business.

I could hold on to the films I already have but then other cinemas would have to do without it - it would soon have a domino effect. Besides, most cinema goers who want to see these films will already have seen them - so I would have more losses.

The back-up films, which I am showing out of necessity, could also cost me dearly in the long run, through loss of reputation as well as income. It is also more than likely that attendance will not be very high over the next few days.

The influenza "bug" may well have upset your schedules, but I'm sure you must appreciate that it has done me no good either. Some form of "fail-safe" system of delivery must be introduced to avoid any recurrence of this situation. Hopefully by the time you introduce it, it won't be too late for us cinema owners.

Yours faithfully

Fred Jones

Fred Jones
<u>Cinema Manager</u>

ANSWER KEY   **Section 2:   Reports**

Practice 3

Stage 5:   Write the Report

To: The Group Personnel Manager

From: (your name), Personnel Manager's Assistant

Date: (today's date)

Subject: Room Conversion

Introduction

Following the request to investigate the feasibility of converting the spare room into a library, I have questioned various members of staff and management and have consulted a firm poll and statistics on the subject.

Findings

Among employees, 53 are classed as students, 40 of these said they would use a library if it were available. Other employees also showed interest in having a library and might be encouraged to study.

The room does not require much doing to it. Shelving would be needed, but could be brought in from other rooms and stores. Books would also be provided by the Chairman and past and present students. Other free publications could be acquired from some 26 embassies, 38 private journals, and 15 other companies. This would keep costs down and the initial outlay would only be £300. Employees are further prepared to staff the library voluntarily.

However, the lighting will probably need to be changed and staff are worried that they will lose other facilities. The MD also wonders if £300 could be better used elsewhere.

Recommendations

To convert the room into a library but reassure staff they will not lose other facilities.

Reasons

a   The room is presently not used as it is unsuitable as an interview room.
b   The cost of conversion would be minimal.
c   Interest among staff is high.
d   Staff could study and get better qualifications.
e   A need is there.

Practice 4

Stage 4: Group/Order Relevant Information

Subject:	Accidental discharge of waste into River Brent.
Introduction:	Report for MD concerning accidental discharging of waste into River Brent, areas of greatest concern, action taken so far and actions necessary.
Findings:	Areas of greatest concern:

	1 153,000 gallons already in river.
	2 Thousands of fish already dead.
	3 Adverse publicity.
	4 Accountant estimates £2m to contain plus, plus, plus...
	5 Accountant recommends £5m to cover exigencies.

Action taken so far:	1 All pumping of waste halted.
	2 Experts looking at pump.
Recommendations:	Action necessary:

	1 Follow accountant's suggestions.
	2 Consult company solicitors.
	3 Hold press conference.
	4 Arrange emergency help to clean up river.

Stage 5: Write the Report

To:	Mr Eric Knowles, MD
From:	(your name), Personal Assistant
Date:	(today's date)
Subject:	<u>Accidental discharging of waste into the River Brent</u>

Introduction

Following the request to investigate the accidental discharging of dangerous waste into the River Brent, I have spoken to various departments within the company and received messages from several authorities, organisations and the press.

Findings

Areas of greatest concern:

1   Some 153,000 gallons of toxic materials are already in the river and reports are in that thousands of fish are already dead.
2   The adverse publicity from this could ruin us.
3   The Chief Accountant estimates at least £2m is needed to contain the problem, plus lost production, plus cost of wages, extra staff, materials, etc.
4   Possible law suits. The Accountant suggests putting £5m aside to cover exigencies.

Action taken so far:

The cause of the leakage - a fractured pipe in the pumping station has been isolated and all pumping of waste has stopped. Experts are looking at the pump.

Recommendations

Action necessary:

1   £5 million should be put aside immediately to cover possible exigencies.
2   The company's solicitors should be brought in at once.
3   Hold a press conference to inform local residents to keep away from the river.
4   Arrange emergency help to begin to clean up the river.
5   Review company's systems to prevent such accidents happening.

Practice 5

Stage 3: Identify Relevant Information

- find out peoples' opinions on training
- training okay - lack of opportunity afterwards
- not what expected
- everything boring after a while
- nobody knows what they are doing
- not really a skilled worker - just a machinist
- day release cut because firm not doing well
- 78% say wouldn't move
- friendly atmosphere
- could earn more elsewhere but would have to work harder
- pay better at competitors
- personne`l statistics
- when people trained go elsewhere for higher wages
- need to offer skilled workers more
- need to make training more purposeful
- need to reduce length of apprenticeship
- need to have better wages and salaries

Stage 4: Group/Order Relevant Information

Subject: Staff Training

Introduction: Report for Personnel Committee on staff opinions with regard to training.

Findings:
1 Present Training
- training okay - lack of opportunity after is the problem
- when trained many move to competitors for higher wages
- not really skilled workers - just machinists
- "not what I expected"
- everything boring after a while
- day release cut because firm losing money
- nobody knows what they are doing during training

2 Wage Structure
- competitors offer higher wages
- about ½ leave when they are qualified, mostly to Forgans
- could earn more at competitors but would have to work harder

3 Friendly atmosphere, 78% of staff say they wouldn't leave.

4 Personnel statistics
- $\frac{1}{3}$ of trainees leave over 2 years
- most apprentices express wish to leave
- when qualified about half do
- mostly to Forgans

Recommendations:
1 Better wages and salaries.
2 Offer skilled workers more.
3 Training more purposeful.
4 Reduce length of apprenticeships.

Stage 5: Write the Report

To: The Personnel Committee
From: (your name), Senior Administrative Officer
Date: (today's date)
Subject: Staff Training

Introduction

Following the request to compile a report on staff opinions with regard to training within the company, I have questioned various departments and a cross-section of members of staff and consulted personnel statistics.

Findings

The majority of opinions given concentrated more on the lack of opportunity after training than the training itself. Generally expressed views were that when trained they were little more than "simple machinists", or it was not what they had expected, or that the work was very boring after a while. Individuals complained of day release courses being cut because the company was doing badly, or that nobody really knew what they were doing during training.

The wage structure was generally considered to be inadequate compared to our competitors, who all offer higher wages. According to personnel statistics about ½ of apprentices leave the firm when they are qualified, mostly to Forgans.

However, many workers, while admitting that they could earn more elsewhere prefer to stay with the company either because they feel they would have to work harder elsewhere or because they prefer the friendly atmosphere within the company, and indeed according to the R&D department some 78% of staff say they would not move.

Where we do seem to be losing staff is amongst trainees - $^{1}/_{3}$ of trainees leave over 2 years. Most of our apprentices also express a wish to leave.

Recommendations

1 We need to introduce a better wages and salaries structure.
2 We need to offer skilled workers more and look at the work they are doing.
3 We need to review our training strategies and look at ways of making the training more purposeful.
4 We need to look at ways of reducing the length of traineeships and apprenticeships - possibly by as much as a year.

Practice 6

Stage 2: Layout

To: The Managing Director
From: (your name), Personal Assistant
Date: (today's date)
Subject: Proposed take over of Social Club

Appropriate headings for this task are: Introduction, The case for, The case against, Recommendations.

Stage 3: Identify Relevant Information

- company needs room for expansion
- plan to take over social club
- no alternative
- land too expensive or too far away
- two sites would cripple the firm
- prepare feasibility study
- question workforce for opinions

Production Shop Floor

- where else can we relax
- 150 workers out of 250 have used it in the last few weeks
- can they give us somewhere else

Clerical Staff

- never use it
- sympathise with shop floor
- would use it if it was improved
- provide better place for everyone

Personnel

- what price success?
- need an alternative if this to be taken away

Senior Staff

- we never use it
- no need for alternative

Trade Union Representative

- workers succeed and then suffer
- will take a poll

Trade Union Poll

- 89% against firms plan to expand into the social club
- 59% for it if alternative is found
- 78% think compensation should be provided
- 7% would like the social club a few miles away

Trade Union's Verdict

- management will have to consider carefully
- could lead to confrontation
- despite success of firm.

Stage 4: Group/Order Relevant Information

Subject: Proposed take over of Social Club.

Introduction: Report for MD on feasibility of taking over social club premises because of expansion plans.

The case for:

1 Company needs room.
  - Alternative site too expensive.
  - Two sites would cripple company.
2 Clerical staff never use it.
  - Would use it if improved.
3 Senior staff never use it.
  - Not interested in alternative premises.

The case against:

1 Production staff very upset.
  - 150 out of 250 have used it in the past few weeks.
  - Would be interested in alternative premises.
2 Personnel sympathise with production staff.
  - Not the way to reward workers for helping make the company successful.
  - Recommend finding alternative premises.
3 Trade Unions - same opinion as Personnel.

Poll shows

a 89% against losing social club
b 59% interested in alternative premises
c 7% think it could be some distance away
d 78% think firm should provide compensation

Recommendations

- Take over social club but provide alternative premises.

Reasons

- Production workers feel their success has led to them losing the social club.
- Trade Union reps warn could lead to confrontation.
- Although some staff do not use it, many would if improved.
- Essential we have support of staff for future success of company.

Stage 5:   Write the Report

To: The Managing Director

From: (your name), Personal Assistant

Date: (today's date)

Subject: Proposed take over of Social Club

Introduction

Following the request to investigate the feasibility of taking over the firm's social club because of business expansion plans, I have questioned staff and consulted the Trade Union's Poll on the matter.

The case for

1   The company needs room for expansion and an alternative site would not be possible for financial reasons.

2   Clerical staff never use the social club as they prefer the wine bar around the corner. However, they sympathise with those who do use it and would welcome a better improved social club.

3   Senior staff never use it either and see no need for alternatives if it is closed.

The case against

1   Production shop floor workers are very upset. 150 out of 250 of them have used the club in the last few weeks. They would, however, be interested in alternative premises.

2   The Personnel Department sympathise with the shop floor and wonder if this is the best way to reward workers for helping make the company so successful. They recommend offering alternative premises.

3   The Trade Union representatives endorsed this opinion, questioning if it was right to make the workers suffer because they have been so successful.

4   The Trade Union Poll showed that 89% were against the firm's plans to expand into the social club. 59% would be interested in alternative, although only 7% would be interested in the social club being relocated some distance away. 78% thought the firm should provide some form of compensation.

Recommendations

The company should take over the social club because of expansion, but should also find alternative premises for the social club nearby.

Reasons

1   Production workers feel rightly aggrieved that their success has necessitated the taking over of the social club.

2   Trade Union representatives warn that it could lead to confrontation.

3   Although some staff never use the present social club, many would if it was improved.

4   Future expansion plans need the support of all staff. If the company is to grow then the staff need to feel that they are to benefit from expansion.

Practice 7

Stage 1: Identify the Task

Submit an initial report - subject "Staff knowledge of the EC".

Stage 2: Layout

To:	The Managing Director
From:	(your name)
Date:	(today's date)
Subject:	Staff knowledge of the EC

Stage 3: Identify Relevant Information

- general points
- younger office staff
- older staff
- senior staff

Appropriate headings for this task are: Introduction, Findings, Recommendations.

Stage 4: Group/Order Relevant Information

Subject: "Staff knowledge of the EC"

Introduction: Report for MD on level of awareness of EC amongst staff in 3 categories: younger office staff
older staff
senior staff

Findings

1   General points from all staff.
    a   57% of staff don't know what EC stands for.
    b   70% of those who do, don't know what it does.
    c   32% feel EC is important.
    d   23% feel EC is important in every day life.
    e   18% feel EC could be important for the firm.
    f   30% feel it is important to establish more markets worldwide.
    g   23% feel it is important to expand into Europe.

2   Younger Office Staff
    a   only 30% know where the EC Commission is located.
    b   Only 5% know how many countries are in the EC.
    c   In answer to the question, "How important is the EC?" The general opinion was "...of no importance, only bureaucrats, we don't have to do what they think, or they are only important for trade."

3   Older Staff
    a   35% feel they know about the EC.
    b   52% however, feel the EC is unimportant and 10% have no real views.
    c   35% think it could affect their jobs.
    d   35% are aware of significant EC activities.
    e   65% never think about the EC.

4   Senior Staff
    a   80% feel EC is important.
    b   65% feel EC is important in every day life.
    c   20% feel EC's importance is overstated.
    d   Specific comments: "I don't feel European." "The EC doesn't really affect me." "I feel European, and EC is a good thing but media don't treat it as important."   "Better publicity would help."

Recommendations

1   Obtain info on workings of EC
    -    distribute it to staff.

2   Organise seminars
    -    workshops
    -    information leaflets, etc
    -    importance of EC to our company.

Stage 5:   Write the Report

To: The Managing Director

From: (your name)

Date: (today's date)

Subject: <u>Staff knowledge of the EC</u>

Introduction

Following the request to ascertain the level of knowledge of our staff with regard to the EC, I distributed a questionnaire among three categories of staff - younger staff / older staff / senior staff.

Findings

1   General points from all staff.

     57% of all staff questioned do not know what the EC stands for, and of those who do, 70% do not know what it does. On the question of the importance of the EC, 32% think it is important, 23% feel it is important in one's every day life, 18% feel it could be important for the firm, whilst 30% feel it is important to establish new markets worldwide, and 23% feel it is important to expand into Europe.

2   Younger Staff

     Amongst younger office staff only 30% know where the EC Commission is located and a mere 5% know how many countries are members of the EC. With regard to the question of the importance of the EC, the general opinion is that it is of no importance, simply a place for bureaucrats, only important for trade but that we don't really have to do what they think anyway.

3   Older Staff

     35% of older staff feel they know about the EC. However, 52% feel the EC is unimportant and 10% have no real views at all. 35% think it could affect their jobs and 35% were aware of significant EC activities whereas 65% questioned, normally never think about the EC.

4   Senior Staff

     Amongst senior staff questioned on the importance of the EC, 80% feel it is important and 65% feel it is important in every day life, however, 20% feel the EC's importance is overstated. Many say that they don't feel European and that the EC doesn't really affect them. Some are of the opinion that the EC is a good thing but that the media doesn't treat it as important and that better publicity would help.

Recommendations

1   To obtain information from the EC about how it works and what it does, etc and distribute this to staff.

2   To organise seminars/workshops/information leaflets, etc on the role of the EC and its importance to companies like ours.

Practice 8

Stage 1: Identify the Task

Present information in the form of a report.

Stage 2: Layout

To: The Tourist Manager of the Arronsay Islands
From: (your name)
Date: (today's date)
Subject: Visitors to Arronsay

Appropriate headings for this task are: Introduction, Findings, Recommendations.

Stage 3: Identify Relevant Information

- information on visitors
- 1989 over 20,000 fewer than in 1986
- 1989, 90% from GB
- 7% from outside GB
- over last 10 years
- problems affecting travel
- bad weather 4 years
- transport strikes 4 years
- devaluation/stock exchange 4 years
- negative local attitudes
- consult advertisers/market research
- conduct survey of facilities
- consider accommodation register
- guide to facilities on islands
- consult travel experts
- consult British Tourist Authority
- recommendations

Stage 4: Group/Order Relevant Information

Subject: Visitors to Arronsay

Introduction: Report for Tourist Manager on visitors to Arronsay, people questioned, organisations consulted, survey conducted.

Findings:

1   Visitors to Arronsay declined by over 20,000 in the last three years - 1989 little better than 1980.

2   90% visitors from GB.

3   7% from outside GB - 3% on business.

4   Many problems affecting holidays in Arronsay.

5   Over past 10 years.
    a   Bad weather on 4 occasions.
    b   Transport strikes 4 times.
    c   Devaluation/stock exchange/currency 4 years.

6   Locals not interested in visitors or change.

7   Consulted advertisers/market research to help.

8   Consulted travel experts/package holidays.

9   Consulted British Tourist Authority on publicity.

10 Conducted survey of facilities.

Recommendations

1   Consider accommodation register and guide to entertainment facilities, etc in Arronsay.

2   Weather problem - stress what Arronsay has to offer.

3   Need guidance to promote the Islands.

Stage 5: Write the Report

To: The Tourist Manager for the Arronsay Islands
From: (your name)
Date: (today's date)
Subject: <u>Visitors to Arronsay</u>

Introduction

Following the request to collate information about visitors to the islands, I have spoken to visitors, to locals, consulted statistics from various sources, conducted a survey of Arronsay institutions to see what they offer and consulted various travel agents and organisations.

Findings

1   Visitors to Arronsay have declined by over 20,000 in the last 3 years, and the 1989 figure is only slightly higher than the 1980 figure. Some 90% of present visitors come from GB with only 7% from outside GB (the remaining 3% are on business).

2   Over the last 10 years there have been many problems affecting visitors to Arronsay. In 1989, 1982, 1984 and 1987 the summer weather was very bad. In 1981, 1983, 1988 and 1989 there were strikes affecting travel to the islands and in 1985, 1986, 1987 and 1989 either the $ or the £ were under pressure. All of these problems have adversely affected the number of visitors to Arronsay.

3   Arronsay's attitude to visitors has also not been very encouraging and the majority of islanders are neither interested in visitors nor in change.

4   Many agencies/authorities, etc have been consulted and many possibilities for help are available, ranging from advertising market research/travel experts and the British Tourist Authority who could all help promote and market the islands.

5   After conducting a survey of facilities on Arronsay it has become clear that there are only a few places to stay with mostly limited facilities.

Recommendations

1   An accommodation register needs to be compiled together with information concerning entertainment facilities/eating out/boating/putting, etc.

2   Professional guidance is needed to promote and market the islands effectively.

3   Emphasis needs to be placed on what the islands have to offer, eg unspoilt countryside and beaches and facilities for walking, bird watching, boating, etc.

ANSWER KEY

Practice 9

Stage 1: Identify the Task

Write a report on tests and recommend strategies.

Stage 2: Layout

To: The Training Manager
From: (your name), Assistant Training Manager
Date: (today's date)
Subject: Apprenticeship Testing

Appropriate headings for this task are: Introduction, Findings, Recommendations.

Stage 3: Identify Relevant Information

- apprenticeship testing
- summary of results
- maths
- english
- test overview

- discussion of results
- comments from boys
- comments from those testing
- comments from a father
- comments from the manager of production shop

Stage 4: Group/Order Relevant Information

Subject: Apprenticeship Testing

Introduction: Report for circulation to schools concerning abilities and attitudes of school leavers testing for apprenticeships.

Findings

1   Maths
     33% failed every question
     12% got everything correct
     18% got things mostly correct
     5% got oral correct
     graphs very poor

2   English
     orally very poor
     grammar weak
     spelling weak

3   Overview of test results
     5% passed
     3% failed one area
     28% failed two areas
     64% failed all areas

4   Speaking to boys - hadn't expected it to be so difficult.

5   Thought they were prepared.

6   Thought they would make good apprentices.

7   Admitted poor academically.

8   Testers opinion boys weaker than girls tested for secretarial positions.

9   Lack maturity and general knowledge.

10   Father said, "Son thought he knew everything."

11   Management not lowering standards.

12   Youngsters must treat work more seriously.

Recommendations

1   Liaise with schools.
2   Teachers ensure candidates are well prepared.
3   Review testing procedures.
4   See if testing for relevant skills.

Stage 5: Write the Report

To: The Training Manager
From: (your name), Assistant Training Manager
Date: (today's date)
Subject: Apprenticeship Testing

Introduction

Following the request to evaluate apprenticeship testing and abilities and attitudes of potential apprentices, I have consulted statistics of results, spoken to those being tested, those testing, youngsters recently recruited, parents and other members of staff.

Findings

1   Maths. Results were unbelievably bad. 33% of boys failed every written question and only 5% got the oral arithmetic correct. A mere 12% got everything on the written paper right and 18% got most things right. Graphs were generally very poorly done.

2   English. If anything, this was worse than the maths results. Orally it wouldn't be possible to let them anywhere near our customers and their spelling was appalling. About $1/3$ of candidates were good.

3   Overall test results show that only 5% passed all areas, 3% failed one area, 28% failed two areas and a staggering 64% failed all areas.

4   On speaking to the boys it was apparent that they hadn't expected the tasks to be so difficult, although they were of the opinion that they were prepared for the test. In general they thought they would make good trainees although admitting they were poor academically.

5   Those doing the testing considered the boys to be much weaker than girls recruited for secretarial positions, lacking maturity and general knowledge.

6   A member of staff whose son applied for an apprenticeship echoed the opinion of many when he said his son, like many youngsters, thought he knew everything.

7   Management stressed that standards would not be lowered and that youngsters must treat work more seriously.

Recommendations:

1   Imperative we liaise with schools to ensure that candidates are correctly prepared.

2   Review our testing procedure with regard to its relevance and accuracy as a means of testing for the relevant skills.

Practice 10

Stage 1: Identify the Task
Write the report.

Stage 2: Layout

To: The Managing Director
From: (your name), Safety Officer
Date: (today's date)
Subject: Safety at Work

Appropriate headings for this task are: Introduction, Findings, Recommendations.

Stage 3: Identify Relevant Information

- report on safety
- need to hold safety courses
- expect people to be trained
- piece work monotonous
- married women at risk most
- so warm - just fall asleep sometimes

- older people more careless
- research needed on causes of accidents
- workers not safety conscious
- specialist inquiry into accidents
- accident statistics
- recommendations

Stage 4: Group/Order Relevant Information

Subject: Safety at Work

Introduction: Report for MD on company's safety record, with recommendations.

Findings

1   Accident statistics.

2   1989/1990:
    29 men per hundred
    37 women per hundred
    had accidents.

3   Accidents in all departments - mainly men in despatch and women in production.

4   Competitors figures much lower.

5   Staff opinions:
    - 10 accidents with drivers in last 10 months - not adequately trained
    - in production 30 accidents in a year - mostly married women
    - piece work monotonous
    - too many tired or eat too much
    - too much stress
    - always warm in factory, makes workers sleepy
    - workers not safety conscious

Recommendations

1   Check complying with Health and Safety Act requirements.

2   Need for staff awareness of safety.

3   Hold safety courses.

4   Statistics on causes of accidents.

5   Ensure workers adequately trained.

6   Try and reduce temperature in factory.

7   Look at ways of relieving monotony of piece work.

Stage 5: Write the Report

To: The Managing Director
From: (your name), Safety Officer
Date: (today's date)
Subject: Safety at Work

Introduction

Following the request to compile a report on the company's safety record, I have consulted the statistics and spoken to many members of staff in the company.

Findings

1   Accident Statistics 1989/1990

     With 29 men and 37 women per 100 employees involved in accidents in the last year, the figures make pretty depressing reading. The accidents are spread across all departments but there are concentrations for men in the despatch department and for women in production. Compared to other local firms our figures are almost 3 times higher.

2   Staff Opinions

     A selection of members of staff were questioned from various departments. In the despatch department in the last 3 months there have been 10 accidents involving drivers with inadequate training. In production there were 30 accidents in the last year. Here the monotony of piece work is a particular problem for married women who seem to be the most accident prone. Tiredness amongst workers caused by lack of sleep, overeating, over heating of the factory and stress are all given as reasons, but in general it must be said that workers are not safety conscious.

Recommendations

1   Need to check that the company is complying with all the relevant Health and Safety requirements.
2   Need to encourage greater staff awareness with regard to accidents
3   Need to hold safety courses for staff.
4   Need to carry out research on causes of accidents.
5   Need to ensure all workers are adequately trained.
6   Need to turn down the heating in the factory.
7   Need to investigate ways of relieving the monotony of piece work.

ANSWER KEY
Section 3:   Short Answers

Practice 3

Stage 3:   Write the Answers

1	By providing nurseries and creches in 3 branches.
2	Through Branch Training Officers.
3	A number of processes and skills staff are most likely to use.
4	Third pack.
5	They should take away some of the problem areas Training Officers encounter.
6	They lay down the ground rules for staff and allay fears.
7	Child birth, bereavement, marriage, house purchase, child illness, child education, etc.
8	Career breaks for women.
9	There would be no management.
10	Interest bearing accounts, free direct debit provisions, non commission travellers' cheques, etc.

Practice 4

Stage 2:   Before you Start

Have you read through **all** the questions?
Have you read through **all** the information?

Stage 3:   Write the Answers

1	Dwindling landfill sites and further restrictions.
2	Philadelphia, Los Angeles and New York.
3	Expensive transport costs and possible legislation.
4	It is not just one city.
5	Department of Sanitation.
6	• Newspaper • Metal and glass food containers • Corrugated cardboard • Magazines • Plastics
7	Public education in the area selected by letters, posters and talks.
8	A bin type recycling truck.
9	Public education is essential.
10	The amount of waste generated. • A projection of existing recyclables in the waste stream. • The number of refuse stops. • An estimate of public participation.

Practice 5

Stage 1:   Identify the Task

Answer the questions.

Stage 2:   Before you Start

Have you read through **all** the questions?
Have you read through **all** the information?

Stage 3:   Write the Answers

1   A move away from petroleum and related products to manufactured goods and services.
2   The Channel Tunnel and the Single Market.
3   A trend towards partnership agreements with French companies.
4   A Country Profile • Hints to Exporters.
                        • Agency Legislation.
                        • Forming a company.
5   Information about • Rates of TVA.
                       • permitted additives in food.
6   From USA and Japan.
7   Carry out careful market research and develop distribution channels.
8   Methods of distribution and local tastes.
9   Producers of top quality products.
10 Machine tools   • Medial equipment.
                    • Security equipment.
                    • Pollution control equipment.
                    • Car components and accessories.

Practice 6

Stage 1:   Identify the Task

Answer the questions.

Stage 2:   Before you Start

Have you read through **all** the questions?
Have you read through **all** the information?

Stage 3:   Write the Answers

1   He is hoping to double business.
2   Small businesses whose trade involves a number of small cheques in US dollars.
3   Depositors with lots of small cheques going through their accounts.
4   Britain, Germany and two weeks ago Switzerland and Holland
5   Low cost banking for small value transactions.
6   By turning conventional US banking practice on its head.
7   Small deposits averaging about $6,000.
8   By free telephone calls.
9   The service is free and promotes personal contact between customer and women clerks.
10 Either by wire or sterling cheque sent by post.

ANSWER KEY

Practice 7

Stage 1: Identify the Task

Answer the questions.

Stage 2: Before you Start

Have you read through **all** the questions?
Have you read through **all** the information?

Stage 3: Write the Answers

1   Very little. Environmentally sound with minimal disturbances to Green Belt Land.
2   Wheelchairs can be wheeled to platform level.
3   Approved in principle - first train could be running in 1993.
4   80% from British Airports Authority.
5   It combines the private and public sectors of the economy.
6   Fares will be set at a premium rate to cover costs and a return on investment.
7   Customer comfort and concern for the environment.
8   Both on the train and at the stations.
9   It will ease congestion on the roads and overcrowding on the underground.
10   It was approved in principle.

Practice 8

Stage 1: Identify the Task

Write notes in answer to the questions.

Stage 2: Before you Start

Have you read through **all** the questions?
Have you read through **all** the information?

Stage 3: Write the Answers

1   High staff turnover/low wages/heavy dependence on temps.
2   80% prefer staff with professional qualifications.
3   11% test staff.
4   Julia Feuell had expected that 50% would test their staff.
5   £8,730 better off.
6   They provide temporary or full time staff.
7   Staff move on average every 18 months.
8   British Rail bookings or Incoming arrangements.
9   a $^2/_3$ retailers use temporary staff.
     b   75% offer incentives.
10   They offer 2 per year - but impose restrictions when they can be taken.

Practice 9

Stage 1:   Identify the Task

Answer the questions.

Stage 2:   Before you Start

Have you read through **all** the questions?
Have you read through **all** the information?

Stage 3:   Write the Answers

1   If IFAD are initiating efforts worldwide for all of its projects to take account of the needs of women and to ensure their equal access to both financial and technical assistance.

2   Among the world's poorest.

3   Since 1977.

4   Make loans and provide technical assistance and training.

5   More than 90%.

6   Three approaches:
   • Projects aimed solely at women.
   • Others with women as primary beneficiaries.
   • To ensure that rural women receive an appropriate share of project benefits.

7   The right of all people to have enough to eat and to ensure minimal nutritional requirements for their children.

8   266 projects in 93 countries.

9   30% of its resources

10 They have no legal tenure to the land they work and are often barred from receiving credit.

Practice 10

Stage 1:   Identify the Task

Write notes in answer to the questions.

Stage 2:   Before you Start

Have you read through **all** the questions?
Have you read through **all** the information?

Stage 3:   Write the Answers

1   A centralised statistical section

2   Generally in written form.

3   On mainframe computers using batch input procedures.

4   One or two teletype terminals.

5   Delay in the provision of printed output.

6   They were replaced by visual display units.

7   Word processing, spreadsheets and database facilities.

8   The introduction of laser printers.

9   In 1989.

Practice 3

Stage 5:   Write the Memo

MEMO

To: Marketing and Finance
From: (your name)
Subject: Advertising campaign for Pealson's soap
Date: (today's date)

A meeting will be held on Monday 12th July at 11am in Mr Attridge's office to look at the proposals for the Pearlson's soap advertising campaign.

Please notify me if you cannot attend.

Practice 4

Stage 4:   Group/Order Relevant Information

1   Finance for Research and Development cut by at least a third next year.
2   Meeting 12 noon next Tuesday in boardroom to discuss resource implications.
3   Imperative you attend.
4   Several projects will have to be axed.
5   Need suggestions from you.
6   Buffet lunch provided.
7   Contact me if accommodation is needed.

Stage 5:   Write the Memo

MEMO

To: All Heads of Departments
From: (your name), Personal Assistant to MD
Subject: Proposed Cuts in Research and Development
Date: (today's date)

It has just been announced that finance for research and development will be cut by at least a third next year. A meeting will be held at 12 noon next Tuesday in the boardroom to discuss the resource implications of this. It is imperative that you attend as it is likely that several projects will have to be axed and we need suggestions from you as to possible areas.

A buffet lunch will be provided and if anyone needs accommodation they should get in touch with me as soon as possible.

Practice 5

Stage 3: Identify Relevant Information

- company losing money when reps go to Europe
- insurers going to raise premiums
- too much use of private medical facilities for minor ailments
- Form E111
- same system as at home
- check injections and medicines before they go away
- changing money anywhere - costly
- facilities here
- why not travellers' cheques/credit cards - safer than cash
- wasteful ways must stop or heads will roll

Stage 4: Group/Order Relevant Information

1   Company losing money when reps go to Europe.
2   Insurers going to raise premiums.
3   Too much use of private medical facilities for minor ailments.
4   Form E111.
5   Same system as at home.
6   Check injections and medicines before they go away.
7   Changing money anywhere - costly.
8   Facilities here.
9   Why not travellers cheques/credit cards - safer than cash.
10 Wasteful ways must stop or heads will rolls.

Stage 5: Write the Memo

MEMO

To: All Sales Representatives
From: (your name), Personal Assistant to MD
Subject: Reps in Europe - medical and currency facilities
Date: (today's date)

It has come to my attention that the company is losing a lot of money when sales reps go to Europe. Our insurers are going to raise premiums because of the high cost of reps using private medical facilities for minor ailments. Reps should use same system as at home, namely private medical care for major health problems and state services for minor problems - all you need is Form E111.

It would be a good idea to check if injections and medicines are needed before going abroad. Also changing money is expensive, especially as we have facilities here for arranging foreign currency. What's wrong with travellers' cheques and credit cards? - they are much safer. These wasteful practices must stop or there will be serious consequences.

ANSWER KEY

Practice 6

Stage 2: Layout

To: The Managing Director
From: (your name), Safety Officer
Subject: Accident to Machinist
Date: (today's date)

Stage 3: Identify Relevant Information

- date/where
- serious accident/machinist lost left hand
- name
- visit the production shop
- machine poorly maintained
- too much grease/not in right places
- protection cover had been removed
- oil around machine and on floor
- machinist had eye tests recently
- had a couple of drinks at lunch time
- suggestions
- arrange meeting for all production staff
- Health & Safety Act posters put up everywhere
- make company requirements for safety known to all
- nobody must flout regulations
- no inappropriate dress or hair styles

Stage 4: Group/Order Relevant Information

1. Serious accident on 10th January in production shop.
2. Mr Hopkins lost his left hand.
3. Visit production shop to inspect machine and talk to foreman.
4. Findings:
   - machine very poorly maintained
   - too much grease and not always in right places
   - protective cover for arms and face had been removed
   - oil around the machine and on floor
   - Hopkins had recently had eye test
   - had a couple of drinks at lunch time
5. Suggestions:
   - arrange meeting for all staff re Safety at Work
   - put up Health & Safety posters all around the factory
   - ensure company safety requirements are well known to all staff regarding dress/hairstyles/protective clothing etc.

Stage 5: Write the Memo

MEMO

To: The Managing Director
From: (your name), Safety Officer
Subject: Accident to Machinist
Date: (today's date)

A serious accident occurred on 10th January in the production shop and as a result Mr Hopkins lost his left hand. I visited the production shop the next day to inspect the machine concerned and to talk to the foreman.

Findings
1. The machine is very poorly maintained.
2. Too much grease and this is not always in the right places.
3. The protective cover for the arms and face had been removed.
4. There was oil around the machine and on the floor.
5. Hopkins had recently had an eye test.
6. He had a couple of drinks at lunch time.

Suggestions
1. Arrange meeting for all staff - re Safety at Work.
2. Put up Health and Safety posters all around the factory.
3. Ensuring company safety requirements are well known to all staff, eg regarding dress/hairstyles/protective clothing etc.

Practice 7

Stage 1:   Identify the Task

Write an internal memo.

Stage 2:   Layout

To: Susan Emmett, Seminar Support Organiser
From: (your name)
Subject: Professor Clinton's talk at Industrial Seminar
Date: (before 3rd September)

Stage 3:   Identify Relevant Information

-   Industrial Seminar "Telecoms in the Nineties"

-   3rd September

-   arrange lunch/dinner/accommodation

-   talk on international subscriber dialling and its applications

-   11.30am to lunch at 1pm

-   slides and video

-   will prepare summary a week in advance

-   for copying

-   fee £200 & expenses/Finance Department

-   make all arrangements

Stage 4:   Group/Order Relevant Information

1   Arranged for Professor Clinton to give talk.

2   International subscriber dialling and its applications.

3   At Industrial Seminar on 3rd September.

4   Can you make arrangements.

5   Lunch/dinner and accommodation for night of 3rd/4th September.

6   Talk from 11.30am to 1pm.

7   Needs slide projector/screen/video.

8   Will send summary one week in advance for photocopying.

9   Fee £200 and expenses - arrange Finance Department.

Stage 5:   Write the memo

MEMO

To: Susan Emmett, Seminar Support Organiser
From: (your name)
Subject: Professor Clinton's talk at Industrial Seminar
Date: (before 3rd September)

I have arranged for Professor Clinton of the Telecoms Research Institute to give a talk on international subscriber dialling and its applications, at our Industrial Seminar on the 3rd September. Will you make all the necessary arrangements?

Professor Clinton will need lunch and dinner on the 3rd and accommodation for the night of 3rd/4th September. His talk will be from 11.30am to 1pm and he will need a slide projector/screen and video. He will send us a summary of his talk one week before which will need photocopying. His fee will be £200 plus expenses so inform the Finance Department of this.

Practice 8

Stage 1: Identify the Task

Write an internal memo.

Stage 2: Layout

To: Jo Hammond, Quality Assurance Department
From: (your name), PA to Mr O Dexter
Subject: Quality problems in Spain
Date: (shortly before 18th of the month)

Stage 3: Identify Relevant Information

-   telephone call from Mr O Dexter
-   on business trip to group factories in Europe
-   quality problems in Spain
-   Jo Hammond to get there asap
-   also Bill Zetters
-   need 3/4 days
-   moulding machine no good
-   Jo should ring Manuel (Madrid 259 3786) for technical questions

Stage 4: Group/Order Relevant Information

1   Phone call from Mr O Dexter.
2   At present visiting group factories in Europe.
3   Quality problems with moulding machine in Spain.
4   Needs you and Bill Zetters there asap.
5   3/4 days needed.
6   Suggests ring Manuel (Madrid 259 3786) if any technical questions.

Stage 5: Write the Memo

MEMO

To: Jo Hammond, Quality Assurance Department
From: (your name), PA to Mr O Dexter
Subject: Quality problems in Spain
Date: (shortly before 18th month)

I have just had Mr O Dexter on the phone from Spain. As you know he is on a business trip visiting group factories in Europe. There are quality problems with a moulding machine in Spain and he needs you and Bill Zetters to get out there as soon as possible. He thinks you'll need 3 to 4 days and suggests you ring Manuel (Madrid 259 3786) if you have any technical questions.

Practice 9

Stage 1:   Identify the Task

Write an internal memo.

Stage 2:   Layout

To: Peter Clough, Production Manager
From: (your name), Sales Manager
Subject: Urgent order for J Laval Ltd
Date: 16th March

Stage 3:   Identify Relevant Information

- urgent order for J Laval Ltd
- 1,000 - 87A ordered for delivery 23-03 - (OK)
- 2,000 - 88A ordered for delivery 30-03
- (1,000 OK rest by 6th April)
- 500 - 89A ordered for delivery 17-03 (no stock earliest 15-04)
- production priority to 89A and 88A
- know this is inconvenient but Laval a very important customer
- don't want to lose his business

Stage 4:   Group/Order Relevant Information

1   Mr Laval telephoned urgent order.

2
Product	Qty	Delivery	Date
87A	1,000	23-03	(OK in stock)
88A	2,000	30-03	(1,000 in stock, rest by 6th April)
89A	500	17-03	(No stock! earliest delivery 15-04)

3   Know this is inconvenient.
4   Production priority to this order.
5   1000 x 88A and 500 x 89A asap.
6   Mr Laval major customer.
7   Don't want him to take his business elsewhere.

Stage 5:   Write the Memo

MEMO

To: Peter Clough, Production Manager
From: (your name), Sales Manager
Subject: Urgent Order for J Laval Ltd
Date: 16th March

Mr J Laval has telephoned in an urgent order for the following:

Product	Quantity	Delivery Date	Comments
87A	1,000	23-03	OK - in stock.
88A	2,000	30-03	1,000 in stock, rest by 6th April.
89A	500	17-03	No stock! Earliest delivery 15-04.

I know this is inconvenient but can you give production priority to supply 1,000 x 88A and 500 x 89A as soon as possible. Mr Laval is one of our major customers and we don't want him taking his business elsewhere.

Practice 10

Stage 1: Identify the Task

Write the memo.

Stage 2: Layout

To: John Llewellyn, Clerical Assistant
From: (your name), Personnel Officer
Subject: Overtime
Date: (today's date)

Stage 3: Identify Relevant Information

- John seen going home at 6pm
- when checking overtime - John claimed till 7pm
- reasons for refusing payment
- John to come to my office tomorrow at 10am
- problem of abuse of overtime
- possible dismissal
- paying back of overtime money
- company view this seriously
- disciplinary action
- hear what you have to say

Stage 4: Group/Order Relevant Information

1   Checking through overtime claims.
2   You claimed overtime on... up till 7pm.
3   I saw you leaving at 6pm when I left.
4   Refuse your claim.
5   Report to my office tomorrow at 10am.
6   Hear what you have to say.
7   Consider disciplinary action.
8   Company view overtime abuse seriously.
9   Can lead to dismissal and/or repayment of all overtime over the last year.

Stage 5: Write the Memo

M E M O

To: John Llewellyn, Clerical Assistant
From: (your name), Personnel Officer
Subject: Overtime
Date: (today's date)

On checking through the overtime claims, I noticed that you claimed overtime on (yesterday's date), up till 7pm. However, on that day I saw you myself going home when I left at 6pm. Therefore, I can only refuse your claim for overtime pay. I want you to report to me in my office tomorrow at 10am, to hear what you have to say and to consider disciplinary action. I must remind you that abuse of overtime is viewed seriously by the company and can lead to dismissal and/or repayment of all overtime over the last year.

ANSWER KEY

Practice 3

Stage 5: Write the Answer

```
        12347    Kasser Bank
        89321    Vasta Products International Inc
        Time:    12.21
        Date:    16th July
        Attn:    Peter Humphreys
```

Problems come up in Spain. Mr Dexter visiting group factories there. Need to cancel meeting on 18th. Suggests 23rd at same time or later. If no good then maybe next trip. Sue Ferrentino could go. Need quick reply.

Best regards

(your name)
PA
Vasta Products International Inc, Basingstoke, Hampshire, EE4 6ZJ

Practice 4

Stage 4: Group/Order Relevant Information

1   People are arriving late.
2   Live further away.
3   Cuts in public transport.
4   Regular cancellations of trains.
5   Women are delayed.
6   Monotonous work.

Stage 5: Write the Answer

There are various problems facing Henry Morgan Ltd at present. The first is that staff are regularly coming late to work. Many are living further away and those without private transport have been affected by cuts in public transport. Also trains in the valleys are regularly cancelled.

The company employs more women now and those with children are sometimes delayed or even absent. A final problem is the monotony of the work in the production area.

Practice 5

Stage 3: Identify Relevant Information

- warning
- incorrect use of machines
- dangerous and stupid
- can cause serious accidents
- someone lost left hand
- might not be able to work again
- get to know safety requirements
- wear correct clothing

Stage 4: Group/Order Relevant Information

1 Incorrect use of machines.
2 Someone lost his left hand recently.
3 Familiarise themselves with safety regulations.
4 Wear correct clothing.
5 Can cause serious accidents.
6 Warning.
7 Incorrect use of machines is dangerous and stupid.
8 You may never work again.

Stage 5: Write the Answer

> **INCORRECT USE OF MACHINES**
>
> Following a serious accident in the production shop where a member of staff lost his left hand, all staff are asked to familiarise themselves with safety requirements and wear appropriate protective clothing.
>
> **Warning!**
>
> Using machines incorrectly is dangerous and stupid. Serious accidents could mean you may never work again!
>
> (name)
> Safety Officer
> (today's date)

Practice 6

Stage 2: Layout

Notes need a subject and a date. They use short sentences and are to the point.

Subject: Royal Visit
Date: 8th July 1992

Stage 3: Identify Relevant Information

- royal visit confirmed
- on Thursday in 2 months' time
- 11am - 12.30pm
- buffet lunch with directors
- everything neat and tidy
- everyone well-dressed
- staff alert to respond to situations
- what to say if spoken to
- staff will be kept informed
- great honour for company

Stage 4: Group/Order Relevant Information

1   Royal visit confirmed.
2   On Thursday in 2 months' time.
3   11am - 12.30pm.
4   Buffet lunch with directors.
5   Everything neat and tidy.
6   Everyone well-dressed.
7   Staff alert to respond to situations.
8   What to say if spoken to.
9   Staff will be kept informed.
10 Great honour for company.

Stage 5: Write the Answer

> Subject: Royal Visit - Notes for Canteen Staff
> Date: 8th July 1992
>
> Royal visit confirmed on Thursday in two months' time. Will be visiting the firm from 11am till 12.30pm. Buffet lunch from 12.00 - 12.30 with the Directors. Essential everything is neat and tidy for the day and that all canteen staff are well-dressed. Staff must be alert to respond to changes in the plan or what to say if spoken to. I need hardly say what a great honour this is for the company.

Practice 7

Stage 1:   Identify the Task

Draw up a code of good practice.

Stage 2:   Layout

A code of good practice is a guideline or list informing people of what they should do. It should have a title, an introductory sentence and have a name and date at the bottom.

Stage 3:   Identify Relevant Information

-   use state medical services in EEC
-   in EEC need Form E111
-   private medical care for major health problems
-   NHS for coughs and colds
-   check what injections or medicines they need before they go
-   change money here
-   use travellers cheques
-   use credit cards

Stage 4:   Group/Order Relevant Information

1   Before going check what injections, medicines etc they need.
2   Get hold of Form E111 if trip is in EEC.
3   Use state medical services for minor ailments, eg coughs and colds.
4   Use private medical care for major health problems.
5   Use company facilities to change money.
6   Arrange travellers cheques through company before trip.
7   Use credit cards.

Stage 5:   Write the Answer

BUSINESS TRIPS ABROAD

The following is a code of good practice when travelling abroad on company business.

Health

1   Before departure, check what medicines and injections you may need.
2   Make sure you have Form E111 if you are travelling within the EEC.
3   When abroad always use state systems to deal with minor ailments such as coughs or colds.
4   Private medical care is only to be used for major health problems.

Money

1   Use the company facilities to change currency before you leave.
2   Arrange travellers cheques before you leave. This can also be done through the company.
3   Use credit cards where possible.

John Walker

John Walker
17 May 1991

Practice 8

Stage 1: Identify the Task

Draft a fax.

Stage 2: Layout

To: All staff attending conference
From: (your name)
Date: (before 21st February 1993)
No of pages (including this page): 1

Stage 3: Identify Relevant Information

- confirm conference venue
- confirm times and dates
- 21st - 24th February 1993
- 2 reps may be asked to share a room
- only share with members of the same sex

Stage 4: Group/Order Relevant Information

1   Confirm Hotel du Lac, Lausanne, Switzerland.
2   Dates are 21st - 24th February 1993.
3   2 reps may be asked to share a room, but only with members of the same sex.

Stage 5: Write the Answer

> To: All staff attending conference
> From: (your name)
> Date: (before 21st February 1993)
> No of pages (including this page): 1
>
> This is confirmation of the conference which will take place in the Hotel du Lac, Lausanne, Switzerland, from 21st - 24th February 1993. All those who have indicated attendance have rooms already reserved for them. It may be that two representatives are asked to share a room, however this will only be with members of the same sex.

Practice 9

Stage 1: identify the Task

Send the message by the most appropriate means.

Stage 2: Layout

In this case a fax is the most appropriate as it is urgent. In a fax you must include the following information:

To: Ove Berenson, Norge-Fisk AB
From: Henry Wilson, Western Petroleum Company
Date: (today's date)
No of pages (including this page): 1

Stage 3: Identify Relevant Information

- arriving Bergen in 2 days' time
- arrival time 11.21
- please meet me
- request early meeting
- suggest afternoon of arrival
- must meet all personnel involved
- must receive all relevant data

Stage 4: Group/Order Relevant Information

1   Arriving Bergen in 2 days' time at 11.21.
2   Please meet me.
3   Request early meeting.
4   Suggest afternoon of arrival.
5   Must receive all relevant data before the meeting.
6   Must meet all personnel involved.

Stage 5: Write the Answer

> To: Ove Berenson, Norge-Fisk AB
> From: Henry Wilson, Western Petroleum Company
> Date: (today's date)
> No of pages (including this page): 1
>
> I will be arriving in Bergen at 11.21 in two days' time. Please could you have someone meet me. I would also request an early meeting - how about the afternoon of arrival? Please arrange it so that I receive all relevant data before meeting and meet all personnel involved.

Practice 10

Stage 1: Identify the Task

Write a description for the file.

Stage 2: Layout

A description is a piece of text divided into paragraphs for different points. A title is useful and in this case the customer's name at the top is helpful for immediate reference.

Stage 3: Identify Relevant Information

- Pearlson's advertising campaign
- consumer testing idea
- test consumers
- then show them how soap is made and developed
- better than showing people who are just pleased
- 2-part sequence
- longer than usual
- show either part of advert separately
- people get to know whole sequence
- past evidence shows sales should soar

Stage 4: Group/Order Relevant Information

1 Pearlson's advertising campaign - consumer testing with a difference.
2 2-part advertising campaign.
3 Part 1 tests consumers and shows them looking pleased as in all other consumer testing adverts.
4 Part 2 then shows the consumers seeing how soap is developed and made.
5 The advert will be longer than usual.
6 The two parts will be shown separately so that people will get to know the whole sequence eventually.
7 Past evidence implies that this will make sales soar.

Stage 5: Write the Answer

Customer: Pearlson's Soap

Description of Advertising Campaign

The aim of the advertising campaign is to take the well-established technique of consumer testing and add something new to it. The campaign would be in two parts.

Part 1 would show consumers being tested and looking pleased with the results.

Part 2 would then take the consumer around the factory and show them how soap is developed and made.

The advertisement would be longer than usual and the two parts could be shown separately. People will get to know the two parts and eventually put the sequence together. Past evidence implies that this will make sales soar.

LONDON *of* CHAMBER

COMMERCE AND INDUSTRY
EXAMINATIONS BOARD

SERIES 4 EXAMINATION 1993

Friday 3 December

THIRD LEVEL
ENGLISH FOR BUSINESS

(Code No: 3041)

Instructions to Candidates

(a)   The time allowed for this examination is **3** hours.

(b)   Answer all **4** questions.

(c)   All questions carry equal marks.

(d)   All answers must be clearly and correctly numbered but need not be in numerical order.

(e)   While formal accuracy is expected, adequate and appropriate communication is essential and candidates must judge the length of their answers in this light.

(f)   When you finish, check your work carefully.

QUESTION 1

"I think there's a big mistake here John", said Toy Department Manager Fred Phillips to buyer John Mays at Fordhams Department Store at The Cross, South Kelsey NR9 4AJ. "We seem to have only 350 of these furry animals for the Christmas sale. If you remember, we ordered 500. Better have a look at the order."

ORDER	RECEIVED
FD Buying Toys	*Pandas are the 'in-thing'*
o/n 147963/Oct/92/1:	
500 Panda type animals	350 Brown bear type animals
- spec 2 feet high	- spec about 18 inches tall *Not tall enough*
- moveable limbs *This wouldn't go down well!*	- limbs appear to move by accident ("some have come off", says Fred)
- black and white non-flammable fur/artificial	- not sure about this fur - better get it tested by the local Trading Standards before someone sends them one
- British Standards BS371	- shouldn't think this meets BS371 regulations.
- absolutely no metal parts or rough edges *Why wouldn't they supply these?*	- a few jagged edges too. *Cannot sell goods like this — could mean an appearance in court!*

"I've made a few notes on the goods ordered and goods received forms. I'd be grateful if you would incorporate these comments in a letter to Best Suppliers, Tamar Street, Kowloon, Hong Kong.

Please ask them if they can supply us with the goods ordered within three weeks (air freight at their cost). If not, the order will be cancelled. They will have lost out too on a substantial future order - if they cannot comply.

Obviously we'll return the goods already received but shall expect them to pay transit costs."

Write the letter to Best Suppliers.

QUESTION 2

"We've got to keep our borough to the fore to please the electorate - and make them think we're worth keeping in power - and to encourage tourists to visit the area. I think we should try to sound out opinion as to what this area needs most - a leisure centre, a formal park with gardens or another housing estate. I'm thinking of that spare fifteen acres of land that was earmarked for development twenty years ago but where nothing materialised because of the financial situation which has existed since then."

The Chairman of the local Benstead Council addresses these remarks to the Chief Executive who mutters that there may still be a problem with finance but promises to sound out public opinion to satisfy the Chairman political aspirations.

As a Public Relations Officer you are selected by the Chief Executive to sound out public opinion and **write a report** on the comments of the local people who are to choose between: a) a leisure centre, b) a formal park and c) a housing estate. You make use of the following material.

A formal park would be the cheapest option. A leisure centre or a housing estate would increase the local tax burden and the borough's loan debt. If people want leisure centres or housing, they can pay for them privately.

Local Pressure Group

The town has got very little for young people - we need a leisure centre.

Youngsters from St John's School

Housing is a problem but gardens and a park or a centre could encourage tourists and increase income.

Citizens Group

Costs

Park and Maintenance:	£300,000 plus £30,000 per annum.
Leisure Centre:	£14 million (half of this paid back in eight years).
Housing Estate:	£15 million but some money borrowed or government loan - but will always involve costs.

It will always be possible to build houses but a greater step for the future would be the establishment of a leisure centre or a park.

Local Historian

"This seems like further window-dressing by our council chairman!"

Leader of the local opposition party

A leisure centre would provide for local people - and counteract delinquency. Housing would be a financial and social burden.

Benstead Chamber of Commerce

People need housing first, leisure second.

Local Churchman

To consider a park or a leisure facility as an alternative to people's housing needs is an obscenity.

Social Work Group

Local Opinion Poll

Formal park	38%
Leisure Centre	38%
Housing Estate	24%

Benstead Banner Local Newspaper

Majority for formal park to develop a better borough.
58% plump for a park in preference to leisure centre or housing development
Cheapest and best say local inhabitants when asked for their choice.

Write the report to the Chief Executive.

QUESTION 3

You wish to apply for a position as an Environmental Protection Officer with a Local Authority. One aspect of the interview is to outline new urban developments and you are required to read the following passage and answer questions to illustrate your understanding of the subject.

Answer the questions which follow the text:

Ten Years of Farming

City farms throughout Britain are joining the National Federation of City Farms to celebrate its tenth anniversary. Many special activities are taking place on London's farms and everybody is invited.

There are 17 urban farms in London which have sprung up in the most unlikely places, mainly on areas of wasteland previously used as rubbish dumps. Differences in their funding and the people who run them mean that each one has a character of its own although their basic aim is the same - 'the development of local land for the use of the local community'.

These 'open air social clubs' as they call themselves will be spinning and weaving, throwing pots, sheep shearing and the rest, during the week of celebrations in May. Farmers will be getting together at Mudchute Farm to launch the week.

The anniversary celebrations will also look forward to the next ten years with a new 'farming the city' initiative which, according to the National Federation, will encourage other community groups and individuals in 'recreating towns and cities that are fit to live in'.

According to the organisers 'It will show people that farming is not just about ploughing the soil and rearing livestock, but also about managing the urban environment'.

Where did the city farms spring from?

In the early 70's groups of people in several areas of London decided to improve some areas of under-used derelict land for the advantage of the local community, using animals.

Voluntary groups got together and shared their skills, and convinced their local councils that they could manage the land and buildings and provide facilities that would improve the neighbourhood. Originally city farm proposals were mainly for the temporary use of vacant land.

The early projects survived largely because they, like all projects today, were founded on the principle of local management. Management committees were encouraged to negotiate proper leases with the landowner (usually the local council) and formally adopt a legal constitution. All are registered as charities and some also as companies limited by guarantee.

In 1972 Kentish Town City Farm took over a disused timber yard in London. In 1973 Freightliners Farm started a playground project which later introduced animals.

From then the city farm movement grew rapidly. Today there are more than 60 member projects in the National Federation and many affiliated organisations and individuals. Each year over 2 million visitors go to city farms, including more than 3,000 schools.

(Source: Voluntary Voice, April 1991)

Questions

1   In which unusual locations have urban farms developed?

2   What title do the urban farms give themselves?

3   In addition to ploughing, what is farming also about?

4   What is the common, basic aim of the farms?

5   Where will the week of celebrations be launched?

6   What happened when skills were shared by uniting voluntary groups?

7   Why did the earlier projects continue?

8   What were committees of management prompted to do?

9   Which playground project began in 1973?

10   How many people visit city farms?

QUESTION 4

You are an Administrative Assistant at the Regis Merchant Bank, City Chambers, Wulfrun Street, London WC2 1NJ. The bank is situated in the centre of the City of London with its hyper-active business world.

You are usually given tasks of dealing with the unexpected. One day a message is passed to you that there will be railway and postal service strikes (but not telephone strikes) from the end of next week. Services depending on all kinds of communication - bus, railway, tube and postal delivery - will not be provided. In this situation you will appreciate the need for observance of certain emergency procedures and possibly the establishment of new ones - as the situation demands. Accommodation will have to be found near the bank (or possibly within it) for key staff who will have to be in London until the strike is over. Regulations and arrangements will also have to be made for not quite so important staff who may or may not need to come into London. You consider too that many more people, including many of the bank's staff, may hope to travel in their own cars to London - and that would hamper communication further. In any event, you would also want to reassure all customers and others associated with the bank, that the bank would hope to carry on business very much as usual.

Tasks: (a)   Draft a circular letter (to be posted tomorrow) advising business associates of the impending problems and reminding them of systems of communication other than the post. 071 998 3333 is the telephone number which people can use when other methods fail - though that and the fax number (071 998 3003) are likely to be under pressure.

(b)   Draw up a list of suggestions, for consideration by your MD, which he might wish to implement when the strike takes place.

5

Other titles available from Logophon.

Business Introduction
ISBN 3-922514-18-9

Targeting Britain
ISBN 3-922514-19-7

Available shortly:

LCCI Examinations Board Preparation Books

How to Pass Spoken English for Industry and Commerce Preliminary Level
How to Pass Spoken English for Industry and Commerce Threshold Level
How to Pass Spoken English for Industry and Commerce Intermediate Level
How to Pass Spoken English for Industry and Commerce Advanced Level

Logophon Lehrmittel Verlag GmbH
Bonifaziusplatz 4a
55118 Mainz, Germany

Tel: +49-6131-611081
Fax: +49-6131-611082